INSIDE NETWORK MARKETING

An Expert's View into the
Hidden Truths and Exploited Myths
of America's Most Misunderstood Industry

Leonard W. Clements

Prima Publishing

Prima disclaims any warranties or representations, whether express or implied, concerning the accuracy or completeness of the information or advice contained in this book. Any business or financial decision a reader may make based on such information is at the reader's sole risk. A reader should consult competent legal and business professionals before making any individual business or financial decision based on the information contained herein.

PRIMA PUBLISHING and colophon are registered trademarks of Prima Communications, Inc.

Library of Congress Cataloging-in-Publication Data

Clements, Leonard W.
Inside network marketing : an expert's view into the hidden truths and exploited myths of America's most misunderstood industry / by Leonard W. Clements.
    p.   cm.
  Rev. ed. of: Beyond the veil. 1995.
  Includes index.
  ISBN 0-7615-0672-1
    1. Multilevel marketing. I. Clements, Leonard W.
  Beyond the veil. II. Title.

HF5415.126.C54	1996
658.8'4—dc20	96-26039
	CIP

  97 98 99 00 01 HH 10 9 8 7 6 5 4 3
Printed in the United States of America

How to Order

Single copies may be ordered from Prima Publishing, P.O. Box 1260BK, Rocklin, CA 95677; telephone (916) 632-4400. Quantity discounts are also available. On your letterhead, include information concerning the intended use of the books and the number of books you wish to purchase.

Visit us online at http://www.primapublishing.com

Contents

iii

Foreword

This is a book that tells the truth about Network Marketing.

Now, ask yourself, "Is that really what I want to hear?"

I can understand if you don't. "As scarce as the truth is," Josh Billings once observed, "the supply has always been in excess of demand."

Well, if it's other than the truth about Network Marketing you're after, look elsewhere, for Len Clements is one who agonizes over getting his facts straight and right and accurately stated.

Len is the classic student. He researches everything. Talks to everybody. Thinks before he opinionates. Four good reasons to pay close attention to what he writes. I pay very close attention to Len. His *MarketWave* newsletter is the only publication I read from cover to cover. In truth—and I suppose it's because I spend so much time writing it—I read Len's work more than my own. But then, I'm a student too. And I've found him to be a deeper teacher than most on the vast and varied subject of Network Marketing.

In this book, you'll find lots of "straight talk" about our industry.

You'll learn a lot about why we do what we do and ways to do it better.

You'll discover new ideas that will help you build a growing and enduring organization.

You'll reveal reasons and understandings that will firm-up your foundation as a leader.

You'll have access to lots and lots of good things to say in presentations and trainings sessions.

You'll have a good time doing this, because the guy can write. Jerry Rubin once told me Len Clements was his favorite Network Marketing writer. I didn't take that as a slight. He's mine, too.

There's an old proverb about truth that warns you: Tell the truth—and run! I know in the past, Len has caught a good deal of flack for taking a stand for what he thinks and deeply feels works and doesn't work in Network Marketing.

The price of passion.

Michael Gerber taught me that passion comes from love. I can tell you this about Len and what he says and writes: It comes from an abiding love for this business and its people. That's enough for me to pay attention carefully and closely to Len's book.

Besides, as another honest writer once said: Truth takes at least two people: one to write it—one to read it.

Enjoy the book. It's a good one.

John Fogg
Editor, *Upline* journal
Contributing Editor, *Success* magazine
Author, *The Greatest Networker in the World*

Acknowledgments

First and foremost, my endless thanks to John Fogg and Tom Schreiter. If it weren't for these two guys, I honestly believe that *MarketWave,* and most likely my MLM career, would not have lasted beyond the winter of 1991—and this book would most certainly not have been written.

My heartfelt gratitude goes out to all of my loyal subscribers who, even after I "sold out" by actually joining an MLM opportunity, still trusted my objectivity and judgment.

To my many friends in this industry, I can only hope I've demonstrated that friendship well enough for you to know who you are—because I'm not about to try to list you all here (I'm too afraid I'd miss someone).

I'm also compelled to acknowledge my upline, both present and past, and all those company owners, CEOs, VPs and presidents I've been associated with over these many years. You deserve an award for putting up with all of my "suggestions." I know I can be a pain in the butt, but I hope I've been a valuable one.

And finally, I offer my undying appreciation to Cathy and Jessica for all their help and support. You've kept me sane through some insane times.

Read This Before You Proceed!

This book will be like no other book about multilevel marketing you have ever read. It will not attempt to teach you how to get rich in this business. It will not necessarily persuade your skeptical prospect to join your MLM program. It may not motivate or inspire you to sell more product or build a bigger downline. And it certainly isn't going to tell you everything you want to hear.

What you will find in this book is the truth. The truth about the state of the MLM industry and the way this business is being practiced. You will find that the veil draped between you and network marketing hides both the good and the bad. This book attempts to expose not only wrong-doing, but also those who would have you believe there is no good in network marketing (indeed, there are far more "victims" of the latter sort). This will include an abundance of information you will never find on a training video or at an opportunity meeting—and rarely even in the MLM trade publications. You are about to get educated on what kind of business you are considering, or have already joined. In fact, in all modesty, I firmly believe that even the grizzled veterans of MLM who've been around this industry for thirty years or more might actually learn something new about the nature of the business, the way it's being practiced, how it has changed, and where it is going.

I intend this book to be chock-full of surprises.

Please understand right now, I am dearly in love with multilevel marketing. I am one of its biggest advocates. I would defend this industry to the teeth, in much the same way a parent would defend his children. Children they would still scold and punish if necessary—because they love them.

The network marketing industry is a child. Sure, there have been MLM companies for more than fifty years, but for all intents and purposes, the industry of multilevel marketing really began about 1980. So we're dealing with a very well intended, but sometimes very troubled, and definitely very stubborn, sixteen-year-old here. A sixteen-year-old with a bad reputation (more a guilt by association, really), but one that's very well loved by those who truly understand it. Unfortunately, far too many of us are abandoning it when it acts naughty, rather than scolding it and trying to teach it to be a better citizen. My hope is that what criticisms are made here will be constructive ones—out of love, and with hope for a better, more productive adulthood for our industry.

It will become glaringly obvious early on in this book that its primary purpose wasn't to make the author a lot of money. Although I believe it will be perceived to be positive overall, it will nonetheless not be a book you'll likely find in any company's distributor kit, or one that will be "recommended" by a lot of upline leaders. This book will definitely lend itself to self discovery.

Don't get the impression this is going to be a few hundred pages of MLM bashing. I'm not going to "expose" any companies here. I'm only dwelling on the negative because that's what makes this book unique. The fact that it tells both sides of the story. Actually, the positive (or just educational) material will make up the majority of these pages. I intend to have some fun with this book. I don't want it to be a downer. It can educate and even criticize and still be entertaining reading.

The format of the book is a little unusual as well. The chapters are very broad in scope, with essays on various subjects. Each essay is a reprint of my "Facts & Myths of Multilevel Marketing" column found in every issue of my newsletter, *MarketWave*. This column has also been reprinted numerous times in more than a dozen MLM trade publications both here and abroad, so some may be familiar to you. Don't skip the ones you think you may have read previously. Almost all are somewhat revised from their original version. I've either updated certain statistical information (I'm a statistics nut), or I may have just changed my mind about a certain point. Other "experts" might lead you to believe their advice and information is all-knowing and perfect, but I admit I haven't been completely right about everything I've ever said on the subject of MLM.

Of course, I am now.

On occasion, I have also removed the names of individuals and companies. You will find, however, that in many cases I do name names. Also, each essay will be preceded by an introduction explaining my motive, incentive, or impetus for writing the article. The essay will be followed by a discussion describing the reaction, effect, and in some cases aftermath, of the article.

There's the obligatory bio of me at the end of the book so I won't describe my personal history right now. If, however, you're one of those types who feel that no one making less than $25,000 per month in this business has a right to claim any "expertise" of it, let me address this issue here and now (because unfortunately, I know there are a lot of you out there).

First of all, my MLM career began in 1979 at the age of 21. Yes, despite my youthful charm, I'm that old.

Personally, I consider asking a professional network marketer how much money they make just as rude a question as it would be in any other form of business. I will say this: My current MLM income would probably put me in the upper 5% of all distributors in this industry. No, it's not $25,000. In fact, after finishing this book you'll probably realize that even being in the top 5% may not be that impressive. I know people in this business, however, who are obscenely rich and don't have a clue about how to do it!

Fortunately for them, one of the few people they did manage to sign up did have a clue. But then, that's the beauty of MLM, isn't it? As MLM guru Dayle Maloney says, It's not who you know, it's who *they* know. On the other hand, some of the most knowledgeable people regarding MLM make little and, in a few cases, no income from it! At least not directly from an MLM downline. One has never even been an MLM distributor!

I would agree that someone who's never made $10,000 per month should not be claiming an expertise in how to make a million dollars in MLM. But there are more forms of expertise than just how to make money. Like I said, this book isn't about getting rich. It's about getting rich with knowledge. If anything, it's more about how *not to lose* money in MLM. In the seventeen years I've been associated with network marketing, and the seven in which I've studied and analyzed it full time, I've definitely gained a wealth of knowledge—and I've never lost any money in MLM.

As you will soon discover, I have many peeves when it comes to the subject of MLM. This ridiculous income versus expertise issue is just one of them.

Another is MLM books that don't get to the point. So let's get to the point . . . .

1

The State of the Industry

The end of 1992 and early 1993 was a bad time for me, attitude-wise. I had just written three exposés: one of downline building services, one about a German-based money-game called Euro-Round (which garnered one of three death threats I've received), and one about a company that was faking large monthly bonus checks.

I had also just written a report on a convoluted, confusing, constantly evolving program where the primary income source to the "company" was the proceeds of life insurance policies taken out by its distributors. Basically, in this business a "good month" was when a lot of its distributors died. In this program, high attrition rates were a plus! It was claiming to be a multi-level marketing opportunity, and I suppose technically it was, at least in one of the several ways in which people were paid. The program involved either getting in with only a $25 fee (and earning several hundred dollars in bonuses, commissions, and life insurance and credit card payments each month), or purchasing a batch of leads for $500, of which more than 80% was paid back to the field in commissions. The entire mechanism by which this was implemented was, in my opinion, a gross corruption of the multilevel marketing (MLM) system.

Anyway, I rushed the January 1993 issue of *MarketWave* out a month early because this scheme was claiming to be signing up as many as two thousand people per week (and I think they were), and I had no doubt this scheme would be gone before most folks took down their Christmas trees. As it turned out, I was right. A barrage of legal actions was taken in the form of federal restraining orders, state-issued cease-and-desist orders, and lawsuits by various other banking and insurance agencies (which the founder claims were all eventually dismissed— three years later).

Right after Christmas, however, I received two phone calls in the same afternoon. One was from a subscriber to my news-letter, *MarketWave,* who claimed he had just sent in his $25 anyway, despite having read my three-page scathing review of the program. He felt the small amount was "worth the risk." The second call was from a gentleman who I knew was not well off financially, who called to tell me he too had just read my review—and sent in the $500 anyway. He was calling to see if I really thought he was making a mistake! He never got his $500 back.

I remember the exact moment, after hanging up with that last caller, when I threw my pencil in the air (it actually stuck in my ceiling), and I said out loud, "Why the hell am I doing this!?" After all, *MarketWave* was not yet a big money maker either. And I sure wasn't doing it for my health. So I wasn't exactly in the greatest frame of mind.

The most definitive article I've written to date regarding the state of the MLM industry was in that same January issue. It also has by far the most negative tone, so let's get it out of the way early. Again, keep in mind my state of mind when I wrote it.

MLM: The Industry of the '90s???

Quick, hide in the closet! Bring a flashlight so you can read this article, but don't read aloud. Someone might hear you. And be warned, this isn't what you want to hear—or have been hearing.

For the past three years we have been led to believe that MLM first was "going to be," and now is "The Industry of the '90s!" Well, we're more than halfway through the 1990s, and MLM is just as maligned, misunderstood, abused, criticized, and ignored as it's ever been.

The mainstream media seems to be picking up the pace of negative MLM-related stories. And why not? We're an industry that rarely advertises in the mainstream media. What do they have to lose?

Some state attorney generals (an elected position) now seem to see MLM opportunities as prime targets anytime they need to demonstrate their effectiveness. Nothing like shutting down one of those ol' pyramid schemes to get some respect and recognition from the people. Besides, the graphic in their opportunity brochure "is even shaped like a pyramid"[1]. And after all, MLM distributors are just "a bunch of lemmings running around duplicating each other"[2]. That's why ". . . pyramid schemes will not be tolerated . . ."[3], and "pyramid marketing"[4] will be under such heavy scrutiny. They may even have to ". . . investigate Amway"[5].

Even the home business publications refuse to recognize MLM as a serious business opportunity. Two such publications recently published lists of the hottest home business opportunities of the 1990s. There was dog grooming. There was basket making. There was wedding planning. There was even chimney sweeping. Another listed the "Top 10 Businesses for the '90s." Gift baskets was listed ($11,000 start-up cost), along with financial-aid services ($12,000 start-up cost). Last year I

---

[1] Michigan Attorney General on national television, referring to the opportunity brochure of an eight-year-old, multimillion-dollar company with over 120,000 distributors (1991).

[2] Assistant to the Attorney General in Florida, referring to network marketing distributors in general (1991).

[3] Attorney General of Virginia, referring to a service-based matrix program and other MLMs that "operate in a similar fashion" (1992).

[4] Assistant to the Attorney General in Oregon, referring to network marketing in general (1992).

[5] Investigator for the Missouri Attorney General's office, before being informed that Amway was a $4-billion, thirty-seven-year-old company operating in over sixty countries (and employing several thousand people and 1.5 million distributors) that has already successfully fought years of legal battles in federal court (1990).

even remember seeing a list of "100 Businesses You Can Start for Under $500." Not one mentioned MLM. Not one!

Likewise for all the business opportunity/franchise expos I've been to. I've visited three within the last year, and although they all seem to have no problem taking the money of those network marketers who want to rent booth space, the accompanying forums, seminars, and workshops are void of any discussion of the MLM industry.

Ambulance-chasing attorneys are still out scouring the country searching for disgruntled ex-MLM distributors looking for a scapegoat for their failure. Class-action suits against MLM companies were at an all-time high around 1991 and 1992 (although this disturbing practice does seem to have peaked). The companies, knowing that bad news travels twice as fast and is ten times more powerful than good news, and being acutely aware of the fickle, flighty nature of most MLM distributors, usually give in quickly. I call it gray mail.

This is a fifty-year-old business with about six million distributors (not fifteen million like we keep getting told). There were about 2.9 million in 1984. Our numbers have only slightly more than doubled in the last twelve years. What happened to geometric progression?

We keep hearing that there are more than two thousand MLM companies in the United States (some claims go as high as thirty-six hundred). Even if you scrape the bottom of the barrel, you may come up with only five to six hundred. Less than half of these are more than a year old with a legitimate product or service. And indications are that the supply of opportunities is still far outstripping the demand.

We keep hearing that Corporate America is discovering MLM and recognizing it as a more efficient way to move its products. If true, Corporate America would be right. But I can count, on two hands and a toe, the major (previously non-MLM) corporations that have formally embraced and used the MLM concept within the last fifteen years.

The proliferation of money games, chain-letter schemes, downline building services, feeder programs, and, yes, even pyramid and Ponzi schemes seem to be at an all-time high.

Not only is the industry not effectively policing these schemes, it is endorsing and promoting them! Sure, the trade publications print the ads, but the publications are not the guilty parties here. It's not their job to be judge and jury. It's ours!

IF IT LOOKS LIKE A SKUNK AND SMELLS LIKE A SKUNK . . .
DON'T TAKE IT HOME FOR A PET!

The interest that distributors seem to take in the industry as a whole is underwhelming. Several very good, strictly informative, educational publications are available to all network marketers. These publications are subscription-based and exist only to serve the industry in general. It's pathetic that the circulation of all these publications combined doesn't even make up one-tenth of one percent (literally) of those that have been in MLM since they began publishing.

So what can we do?

- Join the Multi-Level Marketing International Association (MLMIA) or the Professional Association of Network Marketers (PANM) or both. If even 1% of the distributors out there would join, these associations would be everything we ever dreamed they would be.
- Write just one letter a month to your congressman, senator, or state attorney general, defending MLM.
- Seriously consider running your next ad co-op in a mainstream publication. People who read MLM publications already know about MLM. Don't abandon the trades, just try to get some new blood once in awhile.
- Do not endorse, promote, patronize, or otherwise support any program that is done exclusively through the mail, that promises to build your downline for you, or that offers a product or service that you feel only the promoters would buy.
- Subscribe to a subscription-based MLM trade publication. Several good publications exist primarily, if not solely, to serve the MLM industry and its distributors.

- Don't rip the competition. Acknowledge that there are more good opportunities available than just yours. And pledge that if you should someday leave the industry, you will recognize that your failure was not due to the MLM concept.
- Use as many products and services as you can through MLM, not just from your company. Imagine if all six million of us did that!

Please understand that I don't intend to put down MLM. I am an advocate of this industry, and I dearly love it. That's why this disturbs me so much. It's like watching a sick friend who has been treated by a bogus faith healer. If you think you're cured, you won't search for a cure. MLM is still a damaged product and, until we realize it, no one is going to try to repair it.

For those of you who are looking into MLM, please don't be dissuaded from joining by these comments. Numerous opportunities still exist that do exemplify everything that is good about network marketing. I cannot emphasize enough that this industry has a very positive, bright side as well. It's just not the focus of this discussion. This article is directed more to those already in MLM. It's a wake-up call. A kick in the butt. Big brother (federal regulation) is coming, so we better get our act together before they throw the baby out with the bathwater (let us not forget, Congress came within eleven votes of doing just that when it came to the franchise industry back in 1963). Historically speaking, this could still mean it's a few years away, but we've got a few years' work ahead of us. Personally, I think we can fix it—and before the end of the decade—but first we must acknowledge that it's broken!

I know this article will step on the toes of some companies and many upline leaders who have disseminated this "industry of the '90s" propaganda. These leaders are not to blame either. They're doing their jobs. Encouraging and motivating is part of a good leader's responsibility, and damage control is the company's job. These leaders would be inept in their duties if they didn't try to paint as rosy a picture as possible of MLM to their people. This isn't about blame, it's about the truth. It's about making things better.

Besides, who can blame them? With the state of the economy the way it is, with more than five million people losing their jobs in the last ten years, and with all the advantages MLM has to offer this country, it is rather unbelievable that MLM hasn't "exploded" like we keep hearing it has.

The responsibility to communicate the true state of the MLM industry lies with watchdogs and advocates such as myself, Corey Augenstein (publisher of *MLM Insider*) and Charles Huckaby (publisher of *Profit Now*). It's our job to discover and relate both the positive and the negative. To take the blinders off, if just for a moment, so no one gets blindsided.

John F. Kennedy said, "Ask not what your country can do for you, ask what you can do for your country." He understood that the more we do for our country, the more our country can offer us. It's no different in MLM.

You can't just sit around complaining about how MLM isn't working for you if you're not working for it.

We can do some very inexpensive, simple things to support the industry as a whole. If only a fraction of us followed through, MLM could still easily become the industry of the '90s!

Discussion

This article coincided with a major MLM trade publication dropping my column. The editor claimed my articles were becoming too negative, and that their publication was a "very positive, upbeat publication." In other words, their advertisers would get upset.

I sent this article with a personal letter challenging various other MLM trade publications to run it. Remarkably, three agreed they would, and two actually had the guts to follow through. Of course, one was sandwiched in between a promotion for a new trade organization they were supporting (which they claimed my article demonstrated the need for), but nonetheless, they got the message out. That's what counts.

The response? 99% positive! And the other 1% didn't like a word of it, but could never rebut any particular point. They just—didn't like it.

* * *

A few months earlier, while in a much happier state of mind and in an effort to disprove the notion that I was "too serious" and had no sense of humor, I wrote the following article. It came from an idea I had while I was driving home and passed a construction site just outside of town. As I passed the naked steel girders of what would soon be our new Kaiser hospital, a question suddenly came to mind. It happened without forethought, almost instantaneously. I asked myself, Why do they say a building that's under construction is being "built," but a structure that's completed is a "building?" Once the construction is completed, it should be called a built. Shouldn't it?

This wasn't the first time I'd asked myself such a rhetorical question. For example:

Why is it that when you transport something by car it's called a shipment, but when you transport it by ship it's called cargo?

Why do all dictionaries contain a definition for the word dictionary? Why don't they just say: dic·tio·nary ('dik-shə·ner-ē) *noun* 1. This thing you're reading!

And for that matter, why isn't the word "phonetic" spelled the way it sounds?

Why are there instructions on a bottle of shampoo? Are there really people out there who massage in the shampoo—then wet their hair?

Why does the mashed potatoes section of a TV dinner always take three times longer to cook in a microwave?

Why do hot dogs always come eight to a pack, but the buns always come six to a pack? (I know that's an old one, but it's still a good question.)

Why does the prison doctor who administers lethal injections dab the subject's arm with alcohol before inserting the needle (it's true!)? Is this guy really concerned about getting an infection?

Unfortunately for my loved ones, these episodes happen quite frequently. During one such attack in October 1992, I wrote the following article. Stay with it. There is an MLM connection eventually.

Why Is It . . . ?

If it were possible to count all the words we speak within our lifetime, I'd guess "I" would be number one, "and" would be a distant second, closely followed by "to." Unless you're me. Then you'd probably find "why" right on "I"'s tail. Ever since I was a small child I've been asking that question.

I remember vividly having the "birds and the bees" explained to me at a very early age because of my asking why Mommy had to go all the way to the hospital for my baby brother if the doctor was going to deliver him? After Dad did the honors of telling me the real story right from the start (he knew there was no hope of me ever buying into the stork bit), I remember asking why, after this elaborate, very deliberate, incredibly meaningful event between a man and a woman, did the father always act surprised when told his wife was expecting. Did he forget?

About the age of nine or ten, during a cross country trip, I remember asking my parents, "Why do they say we drive on a parkway and park on a driveway?" Not until many years later did I hear, to my astonishment, that very same question asked of millions of television viewers during a show by the comedian Gallagher.

Gallagher has always been one of my favorite comics. He asks a lot of good "why" questions. Why is there an expiration date on sour cream? Why don't bomb and comb rhyme (a variation of my own question about do and go)? Why is there a permanent press setting on an iron? I love this guy!

I know that taking this why thing too far can get obnoxious. I've really had to struggle to not ask the vendors at Oakland A's games why their catsup containers are yellow and their mustard containers are red. That makes no sense. I've been dying to ask one of the tellers at my local bank why the bank just installed Braille instructions on the drive-up automatic teller machine. I don't know how much longer I can last on that one, but I'm hanging in there.

> Why would anyone buy Levi's Oversized Jeans? Why don't they just buy normal jeans a couple sizes too big?

> Why do fat chance and slim chance mean the same thing?

> Why do all Bic lighters carry a warning label informing you the contents are "Flammable." Isn't that why you bought it? To make fire?

> Why does that same warning label go on to suggest that the user should ". . . not hold flame near face?" Who is this warning for, the Marlboro Man . . . or Cro-Magnon Man?

> Why did kamikaze pilots wear helmets? To prevent head injury?

> What time is it at the North Pole? (I know that's not a "why" question, but it's still a darn good one. Think about it.)

This insatiable appetite to know why has carried into my research and observation of the network marketing industry as well. For example, why is it that if a large conventional business, employing thousands of people, goes bankrupt or is on the verge of closing, its employees, and many times the company itself, are pitied and people root for the company to survive? But if an MLM company, employing just as many honest, hard-working people shuts down, it's a scam? Every time.

Why do ex-employees of closed companies usually see themselves as unlucky, or victims of the economy, whereas ex-distributors for closed MLMs consider themselves "ripped off," or victims of the company, or the MLM concept?

Along the same lines, why is it that if a car, real-estate or insurance salesperson fails, he or she just wasn't a good salesperson? But if an MLM distributor fails, it wasn't a good product, company, or compensation plan?

Why is it that if you create a company hierarchy where all those at the bottom can only succeed by climbing over those above them, and those above are doing everything they can to make sure that those below stay below, this is considered a legal, legitimate pursuit of the "free enterprise" system? If, however, you create the exact same hierarchy, but allow those at the bottom to create, and be at the top of, their own hierarchies, with unlimited support, training, and encouragement from all those above them, this is considered a "pyramid scheme"?

Why is it that many states conduct lotteries that take in tens of millions of dollars more than they pay out—mostly from the middle and lower class—which have a one-in-ten-million chance of winning, but these same states will investigate, file suit, and even shut down some MLM opportunities because they employ a "luck factor?"

Why is it that any other kind of business that involves sales can induce and entice prospective salespeople to join their company by displaying the earnings of their top salespeople and openly discussing the "income potential" of the compensation plan, but it's considered "illegal" in network marketing?

I want to clarify something about that last question. I'm not an advocate of high earnings claims in MLM. But nonetheless, it infuriates me to hear stories of top distributors being prosecuted for displaying evidence of their incomes, even with a stern disclaimer. Prosecuted for telling the truth!

"Why ask why?" the beer commercial asks.

Sometimes for fun, and sometimes—to know the answer!

Discussion

There is a *huge* difference between believing something and knowing something. To believe that your opportunity has the most lucrative compensation plan, or the best products, or the most financially stable company, is great—but it's not the same as knowing it. And this will come through in your presentation.

When you believe something, you recognize that while it may or may not be true, you just personally believe it is. When you know something, you know it. There is no question.

For example, I personally believe there was no second gunman on the grassy knoll, but there was a conspiracy in the assassination of John Kennedy. I accept the fact that there is evidence to the contrary on both counts, and I may be wrong. I just don't believe I am. Now, if I had been standing in Daley Plaza back in 1963 and been looking up at the grassy knoll at the time the shots were fired and no one was standing there, then I would no longer believe there was no gunman there—I would absolutely know it!

Asking why, or any type of question (who, when, where . . .) allows you to gain knowledge about your opportunity. The more you know, the more you know.

*   *   *

MLM has become a real dog-eat-dog world. There is so much competition for distributors nowadays that many of them will say or do whatever they have to say to recruit a prospect away from someone else. It reminds me of the old clichéd scene where two women are fighting over a bargain at the dress counter, only to have the dress rip in half as each tries to pull it free from the other. That's exactly what a lot of distributors are doing to MLM right now.

My newsletter *MarketWave* reviewed and rated MLM opportunities (it was sold in December 1995 to the aforementioned Mr. Huckaby). I had a voice-mail system tied to an 800 number so people could request samples of the publication, or just leave me a message. This line turned into a kind of feedback line for my subscribers, or whoever else felt compelled to comment on something I'd written. This is also where I got the majority of those cowardly, anonymous messages. In *Market-Wave*, my reviews were divided into five categories, each receiving a grade of A, B, C, D, or F. A grade-point average concluded each opportunity review. Inevitably, each positive review resulting in a high grade was followed by messages and letters from distributors for competing opportunities suggesting I "cut down on the hard drugs," as one put it, or otherwise give up on the MLM analysis business because I "don't have a clue." Many went so far as to explain all the reasons why that other MLM opportunity, why every other opportunity for that matter, should be a D+ at best.

Today, this internal MLM bashing appears to be increasing to a fever pitch. The result was this article:

The MLM Stigma: Are We Our Own Worst Enemies?

Have you ever lived next door to a couple who fought every single night? Night after night? She's screaming, he's cursing, the kids are crying, dishes are breaking, sirens approach in the distance . . . . How would you feel about this couple the next morning, as you passed them on your way to the bus stop? No matter how pleasant and polite they were to you in person, what would your gut reaction be?

What if a business associate from a competing firm approached you to work for his company? The company has ten divisions, he tells you, and the other nine, besides the one he's in charge of, are all run by incompetent lunatics. They're crooked, they are producing few benefits to the company, their sales are down, and many will probably be canned before month's end. "But it's a great company!" he exclaims. "You've just got to come to work for me."

Dan Democrat is on TV discussing all the improprieties of Rick Republican. Rick accepted big-time contributions from the oil industry, Dan states, on the record, then vetoed a series of clean air bills. Why, he also appointed his brother-in-law to a high-ranking government position. Dan is also quick to point out that Rick wrote more bum checks than anybody in Congress!

Of course, Rick is on the radio, being interviewed about his recent accusation that Dan drank half a beer when he was ten (Dan claims he didn't swallow it, but still . . .). Oh, and Dan also had the highest absentee rate of any congressman in his state, and let's not forget that racial remark he made back in

1974 (he told an Italian joke at a dinner party), or that trip he took to Orlando with the kids, on taxpayer money!

Then there's poor ol' Ernest Honest. Senator from Anystate USA. He's worked hard through these many years and has served his constituents to the best of his ability. Never missed a day of work, never took a bribe, always listened to the people— and just can't figure out why they all so easily assume every politician is a dishonest, self-serving crook.

Are you getting the analogies here? Does any of this sound familiar? Let me be more specific.

Many MLM distributors in this country have a real nasty habit of putting down, sometimes with vile excess, any MLM opportunity that is not theirs! Then we all stand around wondering why everyone has such a bad attitude about MLM.

I know this phenomenon all too well. Literally every negative review we published in *MarketWave* was inevitably met with praise by those *not* involved with that opportunity. If the review was positive, criticism by competing distributors would sometimes fill up my voice-mail box. And some of it gets downright ugly.

A classic example of this was an anonymous message I received several weeks ago from an individual who took me to task for reviewing such companies as "Nu Scam, Scamway, Matol the Throw Up Liquid, Nasty Safety Associates," etc. This rather pompous individual informed me he was pleased I was promoting these larger, "saturated" companies, and leaving the "little companies for the good people." Obviously, I could go for days discussing the flaws in this person's logic and understanding of this industry and my publication (if only little companies have "good people," won't they someday be big companies too?).

And the sad part is, I get dozens of these cowardly, ignorant, little anonymous barbs every month. So many people in this industry will rip into the competition whenever possible, even if it's unprovoked!

How many times have you heard about what those other guys put into their skin cream, or what a rip-off somebody's marketing plan is, or how so-and-so is going out of business (even if they're not), or the checkered past of its president.

Think about it. Ask any distributor for an MLM company what he thinks of another MLM company. Tell him you're considering getting involved with that other company, and you'll really get the dirt.

So why does this happen? I believe there are two primary reasons. First, unlike conventional business, all MLM companies are in competition with each other. Even if one sells cosmetics, and the other sells automotive products. They all have one product in common—the opportunity. Second, a person willing to consider an MLM opportunity is still considered a rare commodity. Once you're exposed as being receptive to MLM (usually by joining it), you become fair game. You become the life's blood of someone's organization, and potentially of someone else's.

The first step in combating the media's naiveté, and regulatory agency ignorance, is to get our own act together. We have to understand that we are still a small, vulnerable, but growing little club, which desperately needs to become united for the challenging times just ahead.

We also have to realize that our opportunity isn't the only good opportunity. Accept that there just might be one or two (or 20 or 50) others that are legitimate and worthwhile. When one of your MLM brothers or sisters tells you he or she is in that other opportunity, don't smirk and exclaim, "But their products suck. Here, try ours!" Instead, give them a thumbs up and say, "Congratulations!"

What if every MLM participant made a point of buying all their goods and services from other MLM companies? Let's face it. Your company isn't the only one with great products either. Some really wonderful stuff is in the MLM marketplace, but most people will never experience it—because they would be supporting the "competition."

Nobody knows for sure how many MLM opportunities there are in the United States. I estimate as many as six hundred. When you suggest that your opportunity is the only legitimate one, you malign the other 599, and thus the entire industry.

And don't think for a second that people outside our little home called MLM don't hear the dishes breaking.

Discussion

Imagine what your prospect would think about joining an industry that you have just announced is entirely made up of opportunities that are no good—except for yours. Like it or not, dozens of good, quality MLM programs exist that exemplify everything that is good about multilevel marketing. Live with it.

I was recently asked for my choices of the top twenty MLM opportunities in the United States today as part of a survey for *MLM Insider* (then called *Downline News*). Quite frankly, I had a hard time coming up with more than nine that I really, really liked. Twenty that I would consider recommendable was no problem. A list of forty that I would not go so far as to recommend against would even be possible for me. Perhaps even fifty if I tried hard.

Of course, this was all based on my personal opinion, and I'm a bit on the picky side. Granted, that's still a minority of all the opportunities available—but it's a lot more than *one*!

And it only takes one to be successful.

* * *

Three groups are actually responsible for perpetuating the MLM stigma. The distributors themselves are only one. Certain regulatory bodies within state and federal government are the second (to be discussed in a moment). The third, quite obviously, is the media. I believe the media—that being print, radio and most important, television—is the most important group in our challenge to gain respectability and widespread public acceptance. How can that be accomplished? Why isn't it happening already? When will it happen? All good questions, and the ones I addressed in an article titled . . .

MLM Bashing in the Media:
Why It May Never End and What We Can Do About It!

You may have noticed that a kind of stigma surrounds multilevel marketing in this country. Kind of? Heck, most people outside the industry who are aware of it think this form of business is nothing but scams, schemes, and illegal pyramids. If you were to listen only to the tabloid TV shows (such as the trashing of Amway on *American Journal* or Kalo Vita on *Prime Time Live*) or even the more "reputable" news programs (such as *Nightline*'s embarrassing attempt at an exposé of NuSkin back in 1992), you'd quickly get the impression we are nothing but a bunch of cults. Only we sacrifice paychecks instead of animals.

Although that certainly doesn't apply to everyone out there, unfortunately it does seem that about every television producer and newspaper columnist believes this myth about MLM. Or do they?

Considering all the advantages to starting an MLM distributorship over a conventional business, not the least of which is a significantly reduced financial risk, I've got to believe these media people have more of a clue about what's good about MLM than they're letting on. But let's face it—bad news sells. When was the last time you saw *20/20* or *60 Minutes* do a piece on how MLM made someone wealthy, or saved them from bankruptcy, or how it could solve the unemployment problems in this country, or how wonderful many of the products are?

The aforementioned Amway segment is a great example. What do you suppose would have happened if these journalists from *American Journal* had brought their camera crew into a low-key, professionally run Amway training meeting? If there were no clown on stage claiming he'd rather leave his wife than his Amway business, but, rather, a soft-spoken professional trainer giving a dignified business presentation—would it have aired? Of course not! And if you're smiling right now at the idea that such a presentation would exist in Amway, or any MLM opportunity, then you are buying into the same propaganda. They do exist, you just don't hear about them. They're not newsworthy!

Good MLMers being depicted on TV are about as rare as good men. Imagine turning on your TV one afternoon and hearing this: "Monogamous men who respect their wives, take care of their families, and work hard at their jobs—next, on *Oprah.*"

It'll never happen!

Word-of-mouth is the most powerful form of advertising and promotion the world has ever seen. But if we continue to rely on "networking" to end this nasty reputation we have and to gain acceptance and respect from the masses, we're wasting our breath. For every one of us out there saying nice things about MLM, there are ten slamming it to death. Let's face it, bad news not only travels twice as fast as good news and is ten times more powerful, but the news tends to get worse with each person down the line. And consider this: If something good happens to your opportunity, who passes the good news along? Those in your opportunity. What if a rumor starts that your company is having financial problems? That's right, every MLMer in the country knows about it! And eventually, if the news is bad enough to make it to national television or the wire services, the whole country hears the bad news.

But the challenge we face with MLM bashing in the media goes deeper than just a thirst for dirt. I think it gets even dirtier.

How does the news media make its money? Think about it. Radio, television, magazines, newspapers—they all live and die on advertising dollars! No advertising, no *USA Today.* No commercials, no *Nightline.* How do you think these powers-that-be feel about an industry that doesn't advertise!?

What if MLM were to get as big as franchising, which is certainly a possibility someday. Do you think the media might be a tad concerned about more than one-third of all the goods and services in this country being moved by word-of-mouth alone? That's a 33% reduction in ad revenue!

Now, I'm not going so far as to suggest that some kind of monumental conspiracy against MLM exists. Moving only about 1.5% of all goods and services doesn't make us that much of a threat—yet. This is why the bashing may never stop in the future. The bigger we get, the more effort they'll spend to make sure we stay small.

Right now, our lack of mainstream advertising is only creating a lack of incentive for the media to lay off.

IF AMWAY WAS A REGULAR MILLION-DOLLAR SPONSOR OF
AMERICAN JOURNAL, IT WOULDN'T HAVE BEEN FEATURED
NEGATIVELY EVEN IF THE SHOW HAD DISCOVERED THAT JAY
VAN ANDEL OR RICH DEVOS WAS THE SECOND GUNMAN
ON THE GRASSY KNOLL!

Burke Hedges cites another great example in his bestselling book *Who Stole The American Dream*? When *USA Today* joined the foray in railroading NuSkin a couple years ago, he pointed out that NuSkin (which he doesn't mention by name) was then forced to pay $120,000 for two full-page ads to tell NuSkin's side of the story. It seems like the media is determined to get our advertising dollars one way or the other, doesn't it?

This is where we've got to start. These are the avenues we must use to put a positive image of our industry out to the masses. It still amazes me how much credibility the media has with the American public. You and I could pitch MLM to a prospect until we grow old and never get anywhere, but if people hear Larry King say they should check it out, they're at the next opportunity meeting with open ears! (And no, Larry King never said any such thing, so don't start telling people I said he did!)

I don't suggest we try to change the opinions or actions of the networks or newspapers. We can't fight the power of the almighty buck. What I'm suggesting is that this industry must find a way to buy the time on television and radio, and the space in the newspapers, and present the other side of the story ourselves. If we wait for the media to do it on its own, no MLM herbal/amino acid product in the world will keep us alive long enough to see it happen.

So, who's going to do it?

Few companies will. Most MLM operations don't have advertising budgets, remember?

No MLM support organization is going to. Most I know are having enough trouble paying rent on their offices, let alone paying for a sixty-second spot on national TV.

No trade organization is going to. The Direct Selling Association still doesn't seem to take MLM seriously enough, and our two MLM-specific trade organizations are years away from achieving the financial means to pull this off effectively.

A wealthy distributor? You've got to be kidding.

An MLM publication? Trust me—no chance.

A generic lead-generation service? It's possible, but I'm no longer confident there's one committed enough to take it this far.

Hmmmm. Who's left?

It's *us*! And no, I don't mean the magazine, I mean you and me. The six-and-some-odd-million of us who really need to have this media-created veil lifted from the faces of the masses.

I wrote a column a few months back called "Crazy Ideas That Just Might Save MLM" [which does not appear in this book]. Well, here's another one. How about one of our trade organizations, or even an alliance of MLM companies, creating a massive distributor ad co-op? It would have to be primarily distributor funded, with the companies only promoting it. Of course, even without an advertising budget, some companies could also contribute, assuming they'd be willing to cut back on a few $20,000 per day guest speakers at their conventions.

If enough companies and distributors participated, we could make some monumental progress in a very short amount of time. Just imagine. Not only would we be presenting a truer, positive, more realistic image of network marketing, but all the media heads would suddenly see network marketing as a major source of revenue!

Just think of all the nice things they'd say about us if we helped pay their salaries!

Discussion

I recently read an article in *Good Housekeeping* magazine that attempted to educate its readers how to separate the "real opportunities from the scams." While I admire and respect the writer's attempt to expose the hype and empty promises heaped on prospects by some MLM distributors, the article was a classic example of the very skewed and biased perspective many mainstream writers have toward MLM.

For example, the article contains a story of a man who spent a year (and a great deal of time and money) building his MLM business, only to net $18.64. This was presented as an example of MLM's "empty promises." But let's put this in perspective. Had this been any other form of business endeavor, a first year net profit of *any* amount would have been considered a major success story! Most conventional business start-ups don't ever turn a profit at all, and the successful ones usually only do so in their second or third year, meanwhile losing thousands of dollars. Only in MLM is breaking even in your first year considered a major failing.

The writer also dredges up the old, tired argument that less than 2% of those who attempt an MLM business ever make a substantial income from it. Of course, thousands make a nice, moderate living, and tens of thousands achieve their goal of a small supplemental income of a few hundred dollars—but for some reason, this doesn't seem to count. Only great wealth is viewed as "success" by most mainstream media critics.

And, once again, a statistic considered par for the course in any other pursuit is strangely considered a sign of inadequacy when applied to just network marketing. After all, less than 2% of all those who ever attempt a legal career ever pass the bar exam. Less than 2% of those who attempt a political career ever get elected to any office. Less than 2% of those who pursue a professional baseball career ever make it to the major leagues. And, of course, less than 2% of those who attempt *any* kind of business venture ever make any money at all from it. In fact, I'd guess that less than 2% of all those who pursue a job as a staff writer for a national magazine ever succeed.

Maybe we should all just crawl in a hole somewhere and never attempt to succeed at anything.

Since my "MLM Bashing in the Media" article was written, I've come up with a couple of other angles to consider. Rather than trying to conjure up advertising funds to appease the media (which really smacks of protection money if you really think about it), why not go all the way and get some key media people involved in the industry itself? One major mainstream business publication has already taken this step, and lo and behold, it is now one of the industry's biggest supporters.

That same publication, the over a century old *Success* magazine, ran a very positive (almost to a fault) feature on network marketing back in March 1992. That issue broke all-time sales records for the magazine by a substantial margin (and probably increased the revenue of self-service copy centers by a goodly sum as well). Considering the reaction of the industry to this feature, it amazes me that so few other newsstand business publications have followed suit. Recent articles (mostly very positive) in the *Wall Street Journal, New York Times, Entrepreneur, Home Business,* and *Income Opportunities* have also been hoarded by credibility-starved MLM distributors looking for reputable and fairly presented reporting on network marketing. I believe the mainstream media is just beginning to discover that a lot of MLM distributor money is available, and all the media has to do to tap into it is present our industry fairly and truthfully.

So there are two other angles we should look at. Get some revenue to the media heads via overrides like the rest of us, or simply sell out every issue that features a fair and balanced depiction of our industry.

Personally, I like the latter approach best of all. Keep it in mind the next time you see such an article—and tell your downline!

* * *

Immediately following the last article, I approached the subject of the third and final group responsible for the persistent negative image of MLM—state and federal regulators.

Government Scrutiny of Network Marketing: Is It Protectionism, Prejudice, or a Stepping Stone to Re-election?

Federal and state regulators, such as your postal inspector, attorney generals, the Federal Trade Commission, and the

Securities and Exchange Commission exist primarily, if not in some cases solely, for the protection of us all. In most cases, they do a bang-up job, and for that we should thank them.

When it comes specifically to network marketing, however, their performance, at least in many cases, has been less than admirable.

As a result of budget cuts, many state consumer fraud and consumer protection departments are manned by only skeleton crews, and I've heard that a few states have even had no staff at all! The phones just ring all day (I think I've called a few of those states recently). Of course, one way for these agencies to demonstrate their value and effectiveness (and maintain their funding) is to close down a bunch of those "pyramid schemes." You know, those deals that have pyramid-shaped downlines.

Unfortunately, few federal and state regulators truly understand multilevel marketing. Just the fact that our organizations are thought of as being pyramidal in shape is a classic example. Our organizations are in fact diamond shaped, where the levels with the most distributors are always somewhere in the middle. The typical corporate structure is a perfect pyramid. The church and family hierarchies are pyramid-shaped. And yes, the hierarchy of the state and federal government is shaped like a pyramid!

So the double irony here is that not only are the attackers of some MLM programs operating a "pyramid" based organization themselves, but . . .

MULTILEVEL MARKETING IS ACTUALLY THE ONLY FORM OF BUSINESS THAT DOES *NOT* FORM A PYRAMID!

Another example of the confusion that exists among many regulators is a discussion I recently had with an inspector from the Michigan attorney general's (AG) office. He informed me that "personal consumption does not satisfy the 70% rule" in that state. In other words, all distributors must retail 70% of their last order to satisfy this legal requirement, or else the program would be illegal. Obviously, this means that right now about 99% of all MLM companies in the country are illegal in the state of Michigan!

Why does this expose confusion? Think about it. What Michigan is declaring is that if your company allows you to only purchase a small, harmless amount of product for your personal consumption, your company is doing something wrong. If, however, your company requires you to purchase 2.3 times the amount you can use yourself (30% for you, 70% to sell), at 2.3 times the cost, that's okay (fortunately, Michigan also requires one of the most generous return policies as well).

Michigan feels that those MLM programs in which the majority of your customers are the distributors themselves are those in which you are thus financially rewarded for the act of recruiting (a distinguishing element of a pyramid scheme). This is an arguable point, I agree. If I were an attorney general, I would want to err on whatever side involved the least financial risk for the distributor. Besides, wholesale buying clubs are perfectly legal. Why shouldn't they be network marketed?

Other states have also invoked this 70% retail rule. First question: How many times have distributors been hurt by buying more products than they can use or sell? Answer: Tens of thousands. Next question: How many have been hurt by buying only what they can comfortably consume themselves? Answer: None. Last question: Isn't it the job of these agencies to prevent people from getting hurt?

In my conversations over the years with various regulators I have found that a prejudice toward MLM pervades many of these agencies. Prejudice means to pre-judge. Many regulators do seem to have a negative attitude toward MLM operations going into an investigation. I remember speaking to a Florida AG investigator back in 1991 regarding their upcoming investigation into the NuSkin opportunity [since resolved]. He likened NuSkin distributors to "a bunch of lemmings running around duplicating each other." I'll bet NuSkin received a very fair and non-biased evaluation, don't you think?

Let's move on to what I believe may be one of the greatest injustices and abuses of our industry—using MLM companies as free publicity. As a way of getting an elected regulator, senator, or congressman in front of their electorate, in a positive light, for the purpose of public recognition—and thus their votes.

Maybe I'm being paranoid, but tell me if there is a peculiar pattern forming here.

Let's go back to 1971. Two of the most prominent MLM operations then were Culture Farms and Holiday Magic (by "most prominent" I mean getting the most attention, not necessarily largest or oldest). The two MLM operations that received the most regulatory attack around that time were Holiday Magic and Culture Farms. In fact, they were both eventually closed down for being illegal pyramid schemes.

In 1975, Amway was really beginning to take off and could easily be considered the "most prominent" company of that year. That same year, the FTC filed charges against Amway accusing it of being an illegal pyramid. Not until four years later did Amway win the right to exist, and a body of law was formed that distinguished between illegal pyramids and legal multilevel operations.

Nineteen eighty-three was the year that Herbalife really exploded and it was unquestionably the "most prominent" MLM opportunity of that time. Beginning in late 1982 and throughout 1983, Herbalife came under perpetual attack by both state and federal regulators, culminating in a senate subcommittee hearing in 1984.

Arguably the "most prominent" MLM operation of 1987 was National Safety Associates (NSA). The mid- to late 1980s were NSA's prime years, and the first actions were taken against it in 1987, peaking in 1991 with actions filed by ten states.

Picking the "most prominent" MLM company of 1991 is a slam dunk. NuSkin began one of the most momentous growth phases ever witnessed in the history of MLM during that year. It also got one of the worst regulatory beatings as well (which the media was quick to pick up on, of course). The genesis of the NuSkin attack seems to be, once again, the state of Michigan, whose attorney general was allowed to punch away at it practically unimpeded in front of a national *Nightline* audience of millions. He was, by the way, re-elected the following year.

If you haven't figured out the pattern yet, that last line was a big hint. The most important year in a campaign for re-election is not the year of the election, it's the previous year; wouldn't you agree? That's when the candidate really needs to build his reputation, recognition, and credibility. Notice that . . .

IN EVERY PRE-ELECTION YEAR OTHER THAN 1979, WHICHEVER MLM COMPANY WAS THE "MOST PROMINENT" WAS ALSO THE MOST ATTACKED!

Coincidence? Maybe.

Why not 1979 then, you might be asking. Well, that was the year of the final Amway decision, remember? That would have been, politically speaking, one of the worst years to attack an MLM company based on its legality or legitimacy.

It has been suggested by some old-time MLMers that I might be stretching it a bit by going back as far as 1971. But the real test is going to be what happens in 1995! If my theory holds true, this year you'll start seeing MLM companies advertising the fact that they're *not* going to be the "company of the '90s," or that they are not the "fastest growing" company in history. You may even see distributors having conversations like this:

> "Hey, you guys said you were the 'premier' MLM opportunity!"
>
> "Yeah, but you said you were 'exploding across North America!'"
>
> "We're not exploding. You're exploding!"
>
> "Get out of here. People are joining your company in droves."
>
> "You say that publicly and we'll sue!"

But seriously, it will be very interesting to see what happens to the "most prominent" companies this year. If you think your company is going to be one of them, better make sure it's squeaky clean.

Of course, we all think our company is going to be the biggest, hottest deal around, don't we? I wonder what all the elected regulators would do if we all made our programs squeaky clean?

Discussion

Several states are actually considered to be very MLM friendly, such as California, Utah, New Mexico, and Arizona. I've had a couple good experiences with the AG's office of Washington since this article was written as well (it was the first time I ever heard an attorney general laugh. Yes, they are human!). Others have shown signs of some open-mindedness and discretion as well recently. And I shouldn't pick on Michigan so much. It seems to have the reputation as being the state where MLM companies go to die. Actually, I liken their attorney general's office to a hive of yellow-jackets. They sting like crazy, but they rarely kill.

I had an interesting conversation with a representative of the Nevada AG's office recently. When I inquired as to the legality of a certain type of MLM plan, she began to lecture me on the difference between a "legal" MLM operation and a "pyramid." I already knew what she was telling me, but it was wonderful to hear nonetheless.

Of course, 1995 has come and gone since this article was written. Although three companies did experience significant growth, and to varying degrees did come under scrutiny by some states, they managed to make it through unscathed. But a fourth, and potentially "most prominent" company, called Gold Unlimited, didn't even make it halfway through. Gold Unlimited claimed a distributor total of 94,000 by April (up from 20,000 just four months earlier). All state actions (and there were several) were dropped in June when postal authorities placed a federal restraining order on Gold Unlimited, thus finishing off what state regulators had already started.

Granted, Gold Unlimited was an easy, and perhaps worthy, target (as most gold and silver deals are), and I agree it is debatable whether the most-prominent-pre-election-year-company-curse kept its streak alive. Either way, 1999 should be a very interesting year.

Personally, I think government acceptance will happen as soon as they (or we) figure out what's in it for them. MLM programs are very popular fund raisers for charitable organizations and churches—why not political causes? And how about a network marketed state lottery? Or, how about just building the industry to a size where the total number of distributors constitutes a significant number of registered voters? We'll sure get some regulatory cooperation then—especially before election years!

* * *

If you're not totally bummed out by now, let me throw one more little essay I wrote at you, then I promise I'll lighten things up a bit. This next subject, however, I personally feel is the greatest challenge of all to this industry's long-term success and viability. It's not pretty, but it needs to be said.

MLM Start-Ups: Are They Strangling the Industry?

In Economics 101, they teach you about one of the most basic principles of economics—supply and demand. Here's a little economics lesson as it pertains to MLM. I promise I won't bore you.

In early 1991, I did a survey of MLM companies to try to determine the true number of MLM distributors in the United States. I came up with 6.1 million, and I counted a lot of people twice, I'm sure. In late 1995 I did another rough count and came up with 6.8 million. An 11.5% increase. The estimated number of MLM companies went from about 180 to 490, however. A 172% increase! The result? The average downline is 59% smaller today than it was five years ago.

For most of 1992 through early 1994, I offered my services as an MLM consultant, specializing in comp plan design. Most of my clients have been start-ups. I no longer offer that service, except for casual phone consultation. And even then, I play the role of devil's advocate almost exclusively. You see, I can no longer in good conscience support or assist people who are about to add more to the supply of MLM opportunities in an industry where the supply is already far outstripping the demand.

MLM veteran Art Meakin once suggested to me that the minimum number of distributors necessary to maintain an MLM operation on a base level (just keep it in business) was about four thousand. I concur with that number. In 1995, I was contacted by more than 150 potential clients looking to start up their own MLM operations. And, I'm not even close to being one of the major players in the MLM start-up consulting business. I expect the Alf Whites, Rod Cooks, Debbi Ballards, and Doris Woods of the industry are getting many times more business in this area than I am.

So it looks like, if I were to estimate that four hundred companies will try to launch this year, I might be a bit conservative (quadruple that, maybe). So if those four hundred companies need at least four thousand distributors, they will need 1.6 million new distributors to join MLM this year just to barely survive. Let me put this in perspective.

Two thousand people are laid off from their jobs each day in this country. Even if that number were to double, and every single one of them were to join one of those four hundred new MLM companies, every single day of the year, we would still need to find another 140,000 new distributors just to keep those companies in business—and that's not even counting what we'll need to replace all of those who leave the existing six hundred-plus companies—let alone allow them to grow.

It pains me to say this, but the estimated number of distributors in MLM was 6.5 million in 1993 and 1994, and there was "only" a three-hundred-thousand net increase in 1995. In fact, I suspect this industry may have suffered a slight net loss in 1994. Every year for the past several years, one or two major forces in MLM have successfully brought tons of fresh blood into the industry. NuSkin in 1991. Melaleuca in 1992. Quorum in 1993. And there were others.

But who in 1994 and 1995? A couple companies claimed huge numbers, but that's all they were—numbers. They had no

distributor enrollment fees and absurd retail pricing (so customers would always become distributors), and rarely purged
their inactive distributors. So their claims of more than one
hundred thousand "distributors" could have more accurately
described the number of "purchasers" in 1994. Still not bad,
but based on the standard industry definition of "distributor"
(those who at least have the intention of recruiting and retailing some amount of product), these companies actually
brought in a fraction of what they have claimed.

Why didn't it happen? Why was there no blockbuster company in 1994 or 1995?

Instead, we saw several heavyweight MLM companies take
major hits. Two or three of what I believed to be the best up-
and-comers also stumbled (more like shot themselves in the
foot, really).

Nope, 1994 was not a great year for MLM. Although 1995
was a decent sales year, it was only a moderate to poor growth
year as far as active participants.

So . . . let's throw in another four hundred companies and
spread those 6.8 million distributors even thinner. That should
help.

But seriously. What's the answer?

If it's done right, the rest of this decade has the potential to
be one of the greatest periods in MLM history. September 1995
marked the fiftieth birthday of network marketing. Of course,
our golden anniversary came and went with little fanfare, but
still it's hard to deny that there must be something right about
an industry that's survived for this long in spite of it all. Like
franchising in the early 1960s, we've taken our lumps and come
out better for the wear. With corporate downsizing and the
massive migration toward home-based businesses (forty-seven
million as of December 1995, a 50% increase from 1989) what
better timing could there be to expose the good side of this
industry to the masses? Hopefully massive numbers of those
masses will join us en masse. We're going to need them.

When I broached the subject of more tangible solutions
in *MarketWave,* I suggested there should be some kind of

regulation of the number of MLM companies. Or at least some strenuous screening process. Or, how about requiring a $100,000 bond? That should take out the garbage. Imagine—if there were half as many companies, the average downline would be twice as big.

When I first made these suggestions, I caught some heat for being un-American. It was a restriction of free trade. Fine. You can restrict it and thrive, or expand it and dive. We could constitutionally right ourselves right out of a business.

But it'll never happen, of course. So it's a moot point. We will continue to see ads telling us to stop wasting our time with "penny-ante deals" and start our own MLM companies (because they "always make money") for as long as there are MLM publications that will take their money. And disgruntled, unsuccessful MLM distributors will continue to buy into the pitch and start MLM companies from their kitchen tables. And large numbers of MLM companies will continue to launch with no clue about what's required to be legally set up in all fifty states—thus be operating illegally.

Why be an MLM company owner anyway? The whole beauty of network marketing was that you could start your own business without all the headaches and challenges faced by most conventional company owners. No payroll taxes, no legal hassles, no office to staff, no product development, and so on. As an MLM company owner, however, you not only have to perform all the same chores as any other company owner, but you have twice as much to worry about!

The typical employee-company relationship is one in which the employee relies on the company for his or her livelihood. Employees can't just pick up and leave and get another job anyplace they want. That's not the case in MLM. The company relies on the distributor! And most distributors know it. If things aren't perfect, your "employees" just might take one of those other ten job offers they're getting every day. Imagine the pressure on the company.

If I did ever start my own company, it would have a full-blown computer system with all the bells and whistles in place from day one, a full stock of inventory of at least twenty-five quality products—and a million bucks in the bank!

One company that tried to launch recently didn't even have a computer. Management was keeping track of its company genealogy with a big chart on the wall!

So what drives so many people, mainly ex-distributors, to want to start their own MLM companies? It can't be the income. Many network marketers make far more than the owners of their companies do. The income potential is at least equal. Perhaps it's the idea that nobody is doing it right and they can do it better. Everybody believes he or she can create the "perfect" MLM company. Well, there are 290 million people in this country, so unless you want to start up 290 million MLM companies, it isn't going to be "perfect" to everybody.

I think it's the illusion that it's so "easy" to start and run your own MLM company. Hey, just get some good software, whip up a few products, distributors run to you in droves, and you're rich!

Folks, do what I did. Before you ever decide to run your own MLM company, work out of the home office of one for just one month. The fantasy that this business is easy will be blasted from your mind with the force of a twenty-megaton thermonuclear explosion.

Unfortunately, very few distributors ever really get to see the inside of an MLM operation.

And apparently even fewer of them took Economics 101.

Discussion

Here's another Crazy Idea: How about adding another qualification to all compensation plans. To reach the highest position in the plan, the distributor must achieve some amount of group volume, personal volume, and have so many first-level distributors—and work at the home office for thirty days! What a great way to keep them from wandering off to start their own competing companies (not to mention keeping the overhead down in the one they're in).

And no, I'm not serious.

And yes, after the previous article was published I once again caught hell for even suggesting the idea of regulating the number of MLM companies. How dare I!

This whole issue comes down to common business sense. It's simply a matter of what's best for the industry. Sure, everyone who wants to has a right to start an MLM company. We can't outlaw MLM start-ups (nor did I suggest we should), any more than we can outlaw poor business judgment. But I can certainly suggest that we not practice it!

Take a look at the streets of New York. There are more taxi cabs than there are any other type of vehicle. That's why the number of hack licenses are regulated in that city. But, shouldn't anyone have the right to drive a cab in New York? Perhaps. But does it make any sense to allow even more cabs to flood this sea of yellow we call downtown New York? Of course not. To allow it is morally, logically, and financially unjustifiable.

Those I caught hell from fall entirely into three categories: vendors of MLM software, publishers of MLM trade magazines who rely on MLM company advertising, and other consultants to start-up companies. I'm sure this is not a coincidence.

One such consultant went so far as to write a rebuttal article declaring the increased competition within the industry to be a very positive thing. She dismissed the idea of holding down the number of MLM programs as a "fear" based reaction to this increase in healthy competition.

Okay. So I suppose then that there would be no problem if one million companies were to start up this year. Quite obviously, that would be utterly disastrous. So the question can not possibly be whether there are "too many" MLM companies, but what number is too many? I think we've already surpassed it based on the number of individual participants at this point. My opponents seem to think we are well before it. This is one area where I would love to be wrong.

Has this increased competition increased the quality of the opportunities within it? I would suggest it has done exactly the opposite. After all, how do you compete for distributors? Simple. You offer them more in exchange for less. But what does that mean in MLM terms? It means you offer more income in exchange for less effort and money. And this overly competitive MLM marketplace has bred exactly that—a flood of fluff programs with token products that, for a small monthly purchase, will pay you the maximum possible commission. Is that good? Well, what do you gain with such an offer of great financial rewards with little effort? That's right. A downline full of people expecting great financial rewards who are putting forth little effort! And when they fail, guess who's going to get blamed?

Excess competition has also spurred rampant inflation within the network marketing industry. In an attempt to compete for distributors, companies have dramatically raised commission pay outs over the last decade. The first multilevel compensation plan back in 1945 paid about 5% of total company wholesale revenue back to the field in commissions. Around 25% was typical during the 1960s and 1970s. Some companies achieved 35% total pay outs in the 1980s. Today, actual pay outs of 50 to 55% can be found with maximum potential pay outs of more than 75%!

Is that good? Sure, if you can sell an eight-ounce bottle of shampoo for $25 retail, a pre-paid calling card offering $1.25 per minute rates, or a $2.25 candy bar (all actual examples). Although competition tends to lower prices in conventional markets, it causes them to rise within network marketing because the only way to afford these higher commission pay outs is to increase the margins on products (or just eat the profits).

Certainly not every MLM company has gone to the extreme of these worst-case examples I just mentioned. But most do have significantly higher pricing compared with like products found through conventional sources (stores, catalogs, and so forth). Yes, in some cases the "higher quality" justification is legitimate. Some phenomenal products can be found in this business. And yes, a few (very few) have kept their pricing comparable with the stores. But over all, this "competitive marketplace" seems to have brought product pricing to the brink of absurdity.

Yes, this is a free country based on free enterprise. You have the right to do whatever you legally need to do to compete, even if that means screwing it up for everybody else.

JUST BECAUSE YOU HAVE A RIGHT TO DO SOMETHING DOESN'T ALWAYS MAKE IT RIGHT!

This reminds me of a situation that occurred in San Francisco in the late 1980s. I was operating a computer business at the time, and a group of Economics 101 flunkies came into town and opened up a series of IBM clone shops, then proceeded to sell the units for what was undoubtedly below cost (I suppose their theory was to increase quantity and make up the difference on peripheral devices—I guess). The result was that most of the other dealers in the city were forced to drop their prices way down to stay competitive—so now everyone was selling just as many computers as they ever were, but nobody was making any money!

* * *

MLM companies have been trying for more than a decade to find a quick fix to this stigma surrounding multilevel marketing. Usually they try to change all the words around to make it sound like a different deal. Some will just flat out deny they are MLM despite the fact that they pay commissions based on multiple levels of distributors, which is the only real criteria. MLM is a commission and marketing structure, plain and simple. Either you use this structure or you don't. Calling it by a different name, or changing the terms used to define it (or just plain denial of it), doesn't make it not true.

The following is my very first Facts & Myths of MLM column that I wrote in January 1991. It deals with exactly this issue and is as current today as it was five years ago.

What's in a Name?

In its earliest form, back in the 1940s, it was called M&G Marketing, from the initials of the gentleman who designed the first multilevel compensation plan. Back in the 1950s, when Shaklee and Amway first began, this form of business was called only one thing, multilevel marketing. Today, you can hear it referred to as personal marketing, direct marketing, home marketing, dual marketing, consumer direct marketing, and unfortunately, pyramid sales (MLMers hate to hear the "P" word). I've even heard it referred to as "direct-to-market re-sellers," and "multiple-layer retailing." Give me a break!

The most common alternative title is network marketing.

Why so many aliases? I theorize that it has a lot to do with the negative connotation that the term "multilevel marketing" brings with it. So many people still associate this term with pyramid schemes, fly-by-night rip-off businesses, home party demonstrations, door-to-door sales, and really boring products like soap and scrub brushes. One way to avoid this stigma is to make up a new name. I think companies just wanted to present a new, fresh attitude toward this form of business.

While doing research for my seminars, I recently called a Mary Kay representative and told her I was interested in getting information on multilevel marketing businesses. She curtly told me that Mary Kay is not a multilevel marketing company. They use a form of business called "dual" marketing. When I questioned her further about the nature of this seemingly new way of doing business, she explained that in dual marketing you make money two ways: you can buy the products wholesale from the company and resell them at a profit, or you can sponsor others to sell them and you make a commission. Dual. Two ways.

I was still confused.

When I asked her if these people you sponsor can also sponsor others into the business and do you receive a commission off their sales as well, she said definitely yes. Okay. So all these people are "marketing" the products? Yes, she replied. And they are marketing the products on different "levels" below you? Yes. On "multiple" levels? Yes. They're marketing the products on multiple levels? Yes. So it's multilevel marketing? NO! It's dual marketing!

I really question whether or not all these pseudonyms really have much effect on uninformed prospects anyway. Many times I've used the term "network" marketing, only to have my prospect respond with, "Oh, that's like multilevel marketing, isn't it?" When I agree, they come back with, "Is this like one of those pyramid deals?"

Call it what you will, it's all multilevel marketing in the literal sense. If a company you know still refers to their business as multilevel, don't hold it against them. There are many different variations to the structures, commissions, bonus or incentive plans, payment methods and hierarchies of MLM programs, but they're all marketing products on multiple levels.

If anything, I think we should all just stick with MLM or network marketing. Anything else might seem as if we're trying to hide something—as if we're not too proud of what we're really offering. If that's how you really feel, best you call it "quits."

Discussion

I think it's unfortunate that Mary Kay has taken such a hard line against acknowledging its MLM roots. I look at all these other MLM distributors out there crying and moaning about how "unfair" their programs are, and most are a cakewalk compared with what's required of Mary Kay reps. Yet, these women not only don't make a big stink about their plan being too hard, they actually succeed with it. They know exactly what they're getting into from the beginning, and most tend to treat the opportunity as a serious business. They're very professional. I just wish they'd lose the term "dual marketing" and join the club. We need them.

We had a semi-regular column in *MarketWave* called "In The Dog House." Usually it's a facetious little column directed more toward individuals who are in hot water with us, rather than companies, and it's usually not taken too seriously—by our readers or us.

In one recent column, though, I really took to task a well-known MLM company (specifically their president and CEO) for claiming not only that this was not a multilevel marketing opportunity, but the reason it wasn't was because MLM opportunities involve big hype, front-loading of products, singing and chanting, products of little value, and only recruitment-focused "get rich quick" promotions. The CEO even suggested, rather ironically, that MLMs typically hide the true nature of their business.

Now we've got MLM company presidents bashing MLM. Is this a bad dream?!

The semantic game playing that's going on with this company goes far beyond just changing the name of their form of marketing. They've changed the names of every term they now use in their business. Of course, this begs the question, if they're not MLM, then why have they been using what they now claim was MLM terminology for the last seven years?

IF I CALL MY TIRES "LANDING GEAR," THE CAB A "COCKPIT," THE LOUVERS "AILERONS," AND THE BODY A "FUSELAGE," THAT DOESN'T MAKE MY TOYOTA A 747!

Companies like these can call themselves whatever they want, and perhaps they'll fool a few naive distributors. But the majority of those in this industry, as well as state and federal regulatory agencies, won't buy it for a minute. Like it or not, these pseudo-named MLM companies will be forever bound to MLM by an unseverable chain. If this ship we call multilevel marketing ever sinks into a sea of federal regulation, they're going to the bottom right along with it. And we do seem to be taking on a little water.

I would strongly suggest to these companies that rather than trying to saw through the chain, they might want to grab a bucket!

* * *

Many of my past occupations have involved close contact, at least on a psychological level, with a large number of people. My very first real job was a "cook" at Taco Bell. The food production phase of my career wasn't very challenging because everything Taco Bell offered then was essentially beans, ground beef, lettuce, and cheese just folded different ways (lay it flat, you had a tostada; fold it once, you had a taco; roll it up, you had a burrito). My "promotion" to the front counter provided my first glimpse into the workings of the average American mind on a mass scale. And it was scary.

I also spent sixteen years as a professional umpire (little league to semi-pro). I learned far more about the nature of human reasoning (or lack of such) from the people in the stands than I did from the players or coaches. And it was even scarier.

Then I opened my own computer time rental and training business—right on the border of San Francisco's Mission and Castro districts. I'm not going to elaborate, other than to say it was the most disturbing six years of my life. I did more than leave my heart in San Francisco, I left my car, my clothes, my furniture—I couldn't get out of there fast enough!

(A personal note to all Bay Area readers: Yes, I do believe San Francisco is a beautiful city—from high up, far away, at night.)

Enter Network Marketing. Despite my past endeavors into the human condition, nothing prepared me for this. Network marketers have their own, unique eccentricities. Their own original style of reasoning. And after seventeen years of working with uplines, downlines, and crosslines, I've started to wonder . . .

Does MLM Make Us Goofy?

My six-plus years as one of the MLM industry "watchdogs" has involved several hundred hours of reading various MLM related books, newsletters, and magazines and having conversations with literally thousands of MLM participants, vendors, trainers, and owners. Over this period, I have concluded that something about the MLM industry is making quite a few of us really goofy. Perhaps our "herbal formulas" contain more herbs than we know about. Or, maybe it's the radiation we've absorbed from watching all those videos. It could be that pressing a phone against your head six to eight hours a day cuts off blood vessels to your brain. All I know is, something is going on here.

A classic example is a conversation I had about three years ago with a local print-shop owner. A print shop, by the way, that claimed to have several MLM clients.

I called this printer to get a quote on what it would cost to reprint a limited number of back issues of *MarketWave*. She said they had a special deal where all double-sided, eleven-by-seventeen pages would be 15¢ per sheet. I then asked (remember, this is the owner I'm talking to) what would be the fewest number they could print. She replied that they could print whatever amount I needed. Okay, what about ten? Well, she said, they really couldn't print that few. She then explained to me about set up costs, labor, and various other fixed costs. Fair enough. So exactly what is the least number you could print, I asked. She again replied, "As I said sir, we can print any amount you wish."

Uh oh.

"How about twenty?" I ventured. Nope. Couldn't print that few either. It just wouldn't be cost effective, you see, because of those fixed costs, which she began to list again.

Now, I had already tried "fewest" and "least." I wouldn't dare try "minimum." That's another whole syllable. Ah, what the heck, I thought, let's give it a try.

"All right. So exactly what is the minimum number of sheets that you can print?"

"Sir," she responded, obviously getting annoyed, "like I said, we can print whatever number you like, we just can't print that few."

Believe it or not, we went through this loop about three more times, each time with me raising the requested number by ten, followed by her desperately trying to get through my thick skull that they could print whatever amount I needed— except for every amount I requested.

The call ended with me (who my Little League team used to call "Spock" because of my inability to get riled) yelling into the phone "fifty-one, fifty-two, fifty-three, fifty-four, . . . *Stop me when I hit a number you can print!*"

She hung up on me.

To this day, I still don't know what the least, fewest, minimum number of pages is she could print for me. And I never will. She went out of business—just like the MLM company she was a distributor for (Consumer's Buyline).

The logic portion of the brain seems to be most affected by MLM exposure. More evidence of this can be found in the ads we place. Just recently I saw one with the headline "Little Known Secrets . . ." What other kind of secrets are there? Well-known secrets?

Or, how about this one: "Brand New MLM Now Launching!" Have you ever seen an old MLM company launch?

Or, how about this logic buster: "Earn income through the retail sale of our FREE reports!"

Here's another headline I just saw which you can add to your list: "The MLM Learing Group." I mean, how does this happen? *Learing?* I liken these types of mega-typos to a pedestrian being accidentally hit by a train in broad daylight. I occasionally hear about this happening, and as morbid as it is, I almost want to be there to see exactly how such an event could occur. When a typesetter keys in a headline such as "Credit Problems, Money Troubles, Down On Your Lick?" (actual copy), does he not look up and read what he just typed at least once?

Here are a few more true stories from the annals of *MarketWave.*

I got a call about two months ago from a distraught gentleman who was incensed that I did not have a system in place to provide him with a sample copy of my newsletter. He and his wife were roaming the country in his motor home, you see. And yes, he was quite serious.

Another gentleman called recently to order a subscription and a back issue. When I explained that there was a $2 shipping and handling charge on the back issue, he protested that since I had to send the first issue of his subscription anyway, why was he being charged for the shipping on the back issue?

(An argument that has come up more than once, by the way). I explained that there was additional postage, and back issues were all hand folded and collated and were more expensive to produce because they are reprinted in limited quantity. He wasn't buying it. Literally. He bluntly stated that he would cancel his order if the $2 was charged. I later discovered that this guy earns in excess of $13,000 per month in a well-known MLM program. That's *thirteen thousand dollars*—two of which he got to keep that day.

Just recently a new MLMer, who sounded way too young to have already been so affected, called my voice mail and requested a sample copy of *MarketWave*. His message was as follows: "Yes, this is John Smith from Tampa, Florida, and I just read your article in *Profits Magazine*. I would like to get the sample copy as soon as possible and I will send you the dollar you requested. Thank you." Click.

The real frustrating part is that Mr. Smith (not his real name) is the third person to leave such a message so far this year! And that's not counting the two by Mr. Smith himself, who's still wondering where his sample is and whose address we still don't know.

I can't count the number of times, especially in the early years of *MarketWave,* that I would fax information requests or a series of questions regarding the company I was reviewing, only to have every one completely ignored. Or I made numerous calls to the corporate office to talk to the president or VP regarding questions or concerns that I didn't feel comfortable asking distributors, and never had a single call returned. And then, after the review is published, I get a call or letter from the president chastising me for not getting my facts straight.

Actually, that's not a good example of being goofy, that's just me venting. Thanks for indulging me.

Goofy? How about the infamous MetChem scandal? This was a bogus review I did (as an April Fool's joke) for a scheme where you could get paid $6 for every tin can you sent in (because MetChem found a way to convert tin into platinum, you see). Honestly, it's not the fact that sixteen of my subscribers called in to get the address for MetChem (after all, the information was supposed to be coming from a reputable source—me!). It's the fact that the instructions to order the information clearly stated "Go sit in the corner. Haven't we taught you anything?" then asked that you spell out the first letters of each sentence of the first paragraph—which spelled APRIL FOOLS. Fortunately, twelve of them called back to ask that I ignore their previous request. Good for them. The others (and you know who you are) claimed they followed the instructions perfectly—and still wanted the address!

So far, I've received three death threats. Two were just a prank (I'm pretty sure), but the other seemed quite serious. This angry, anonymous caller was upset that I had "trashed" his opportunity and that my review was "sinful." That review resulted in the third highest rated opportunity ever featured in *MarketWave*, and the highest for the year in which the call was made. Wadda' they want from me already?!

Last month I had a discussion with a man who was dissatisfied with the performance of his current company's compensation plan (we'll call his company Generic International). He called to ask me about the plan I was working. I told him the type, and he replied, "Eh, I was hoping to stay with a plan like Generic's." I then explained the pay out. "Hmmm. Actually, I kind of like an even pay out—like Generic's." I forged on. After explaining the qualifications, he responded by explaining to me why he liked the way "Generic was doing it." The conversation eventually went beyond comp plans to products. After telling him about mine, sure enough, he was hoping to stay with products "like Generic has." He stayed with Generic International.

I recently came across a distributor-produced full-page ad for an MLM opportunity within which the distributor described his company's great new support tool—an automated downline and sales volume tracking system. Nothing wrong with that, except that when describing how simple the steps were to use the system he used his actual ID number and password! Yes, of course I called and accessed the system (I'm not nosy, I'm inquisitive). This guy, who was claiming to have achieved great success with this opportunity, had 115 people on his first level alone, but his total commissions earned for the past month was $26! The headline of his ad read: "My 10 years of MLM frustration." I have a theory about that.

Another MLM company I was preparing to review sent out an open letter to all of its distributors chastising them for accepting returns of their weight-loss product. It seems many of them were returning the thirty-day supply of product with only a few of the capsules consumed. The author of this letter, their national marketing director, claimed that customers must use all thirty days' worth of product to get any results. Therefore, in spite of their "100% money-back guarantee" on retail customer returns, the company would no longer provide refunds on unfinished product returned by its distributors—unless the bottle was returned empty! Hmmm. There's got to be a way around this policy. Let's think hard.

A discussion of goofiness in network marketing cannot end without at least a mention of those folks who claimed to have depleted their life savings to purchase huge inventory loads upon joining an MLM opportunity (the highest I've heard of is $120,000). Or those who leave high-paying, secure jobs to work an MLM opportunity full time after only a few weeks or months of success. I just read about a Long Island man who left a $192,000-a-year job to work FundAmerica back in early 1990. Bad timing. Bad.

NGS (Networking Goofiness Syndrome) seems to be spreading in epidemic proportions. This dreaded malady must be stopped before the end of the 1990s, when 65% of all goods and services will be moved by way of network marketing (at least according to the *Wall Street Journal*). Unknowing college and university professors all over the country are now teaching people how to inflict themselves with NGS. Even Donald Trump claimed he would risk exposure to NGS by pursuing network marketing should he ever lose his fortune again. (All of the above statements are ridiculous, yet common, MLM myths. They are completely untrue. Don't repeat them, please.)

Fortunately, despite all of the massive exposure I've had to network marketing over a prolonged period of time, I personally seem to have been completely unaffected. I have experienced no symptoms of Networking Goofiness Syndrome of any kind.

By the way, not to change the subject, but I want all of my readers to be aware that I no longer wish to be referred to by my given name, but rather by this unpronounceable symbol:

Thank you for your cooperation.

Discussion

Since I wrote this article, I've spent two months working out of the home office of an MLM company. I could probably produce a three-volume set of books on NGS from just that experience. Have you ever seen an entire product order written small enough to fit in the memo section of a check? I have. One letter to the president (to the *president*) was more cute than goofy. It was from a nice lady who was having trouble getting her product delivered, so she included detailed information on how to find her house (go down the dirt road for two miles, turn left at the big willow tree . . .).

I also got to handle a complaint to the attorney general of Washington (remember, the one that laughed?) that involved a lady who completely filled out and signed a form to apply for a monthly Electronic Funds Transfer (EFT) of $25 (a standard feature in many MLM programs). She even included the requisite voided check. When $25 was automatically deducted from her account the following month, she fired off a scathing letter to the Washington Consumer Fraud Division. She claimed this company had actually "removed" funds from her account "without my signature." She even included a copy of the EFT paper draft! She demanded that these "dishonest" crooks be "shut down immediately!" They sent her $25 back.

I now have a whole new perspective on the inner workings of MLM companies. I've also gained an abundance of respect and empathy for MLM corporate people. I wouldn't have their jobs for a million dollars. A million-five maybe, but not a million.

For those of you who have trouble recognizing sarcasm (even when it's so thick it drips off the page into your lap), I don't really think MLM makes people goofy. I think most of us are pretty goofy already. Case in point: The Coca-Cola Company claims it has received hundreds of letters all wanting to know the same thing—are those Coke-drinking, ice-skating, belly-luging, star-gazing polar bears in their TV commercials real!? True story.

Just imagine what would happen if Coca-Cola ever went MLM!

2

What We Should Be Doing
(But Are Not)

By "we" I am referring to the entire MLM industry. Obviously many of you are doing many of the techniques and ideas found in this chapter. Unfortunately, most of us are not.

While MLM goofiness is still fresh on our minds, let's begin with the aforementioned list of my favorite MLM and mail-order ad headlines. Keep in mind, these are not made up. Every one is an actual headline. I only emphasize that because it's going to be really hard to believe.

MLM and Mail Order Advertising at Its Weirdest:
My All-Time Top Favorites!

For years I've been reading the various MLM trade publications, card decks, and mail-order solicitations, and I have often laughed, and sometimes cringed, at some of the bogus claims, typos, and not-so-professional ad copy. I have collected these ads in a separate file for about the last ten months. Some I remember from years past. This is a collection of my personal favorites.

To protect the innocent, the advertisers themselves, the publication or card deck in which the ad was found, and, in most cases, the company are not mentioned. It is not my intention to belittle any distributor, any advertising medium, or any opportunity by name. Let's just have some fun.

How to Get 1,000,000 People to Mail You $3. For info, please send $3 to . . . Many variations of this common classified ad have appeared. And yes, the trick is to place an ad like this one and hope there are 999,999 more suckers out there (besides yourself).

No Competition!   A bold headline on an ad for an MLM long-distance service. There are only about four hundred long-distance carriers in the United States, of which roughly twenty are MLM.

$40,000 Plus a Free Vacation. No Selling—No Recruiting—No Monthly Purchases—No Work of Any Kind!   And no chance of any kind that it will ever work!

$320,000 in 18 Months or Less—Results Are Guaranteed . . . Perfectly Legal in Germany!   "Excuse me Mr. Postal Inspector. You can't touch us U.S. distributors. This program is perfectly legal in Germany!" Yeah, sure. They'll buy that.

I CAN GET IT IN!   From an ad run by an advertising agent for an MLM publication. He can get your ad in—get it?

Earn $90,000 in One Year or More!   Pretty safe claim, isn't it?

Build Your Own Downline . . .   What a concept!

No Selling . . . Let the Big Savings Do the Selling for You! Has anyone ever seen "Big Savings" pick up a telephone, call up a prospect, and describe itself?

Don't Think Your Thoughts. New Thoughts!!!   Huh???

Ground Floor Opportunity . . .   Attributed to a 125-year-old company that has been operating as an MLM program for more than 15 years.

Distributors Wanted!   That was the whole ad, plus a phone number. The only thing missing was a reason to call it!

Pays 100% on Level Six!   That's it. The whole 100% on just the sixth level. Ohhh, look at all the pretty red flags.

Don't Call This Number!   A recent headline in a display ad. Easy instruction to follow. The ad contained no phone number.

Hard Work—Great Rewards. What's this? Truth in advertising? In MLM!? Better watch out or we just might start signing up only serious, committed people.

Earn Big Money Working at Home, in Your Mailbox. Of course, you'll need a reeeeal tiny fax machine, a reeeeal tiny desk . . .

Amazing New Wealth Secret! Rush S.A.S.E. today! The system works so well, they require that you spring for the 32¢ stamp to send it to you. Hmmmm . . .

Free Allergies. Sneezing. Watery eyes. Runny nose. And if you act now, they'll even throw in a little athlete's foot!

I Have Thoroughly Evaluated 2,000-plus MLM Programs . . . *MarketWave* has spent more than eleven thousand man (and woman) hours, over the last three-plus years "thoroughly evaluating" MLM opportunities—and we've evaluated about 120.

You Can Make a Fortune—By Passing Out, or Mailing Tapes I Will Give You. Passing out seems like less work and a lot more relaxing.

We Will Place Every Person Who Responds to This Ad After You in Our Downline! Freudian slip?

The Typo Hall of Fame

I Earned Over $10.000 in My First 90 Days! I can make more than that, including tips, working for Domino's Pizza— in my first ninety minutes.

Credit Problems, Money Troubles, Down On Your Lick? That "I" key is just so close to the "U" key, isn't it?

Join Body Wide Today! The real disaster here is that this was an ad for a company that sells weight-loss products. Oops!

History Making MLM Just Lunched! No this wasn't an ad in a magazine, or a card deck, or a promotional flyer. It was the headline on page one of the company's first newsletter!

Discussion

So . . . What should we be doing (but are not)? It's called proofreading!

* * *

Without a doubt, my most popular Facts & Myths column ever was one of the few that addressed a recruiting technique. Generally, I don't write about how to do the business, but this particular article just begged to be written.

MarketWave was once part of a larger corporation that was headed by three of the most brilliant individuals I have ever met. They had spent many years before my involvement studying and analyzing tons of data they had collected pertaining to what I'll call, for the sake of simplicity, business and sales psychology. My association with these men, and the insights I gained from them, led me to discover a key element in the typical MLM recruiting process that was being completely ignored throughout the industry. And it had nothing to do with MLM really.

Another element of the recruiting process that I had discovered years earlier (along with several million other network marketers) was one that involved overcoming the MLM stigma. Unfortunately, I found that many distributors were trying to overcome this objection by trying to force their opportunity pitch right through the middle of it. All in the hopes that the features and benefits of their particular program would overcome the prospect's objection to the entire MLM concept. It rarely worked.

These two factors were the inspiration for this article . . .

The ABC Technique

Would you ever try to pour hot coffee into a thermos with the lid still on? Could you put a videocassette into your VCR if it already had a cartridge in it? Of course not. Unfortunately, the way that most people prospect for MLM partners makes about as much sense.

For many years, we've all been taught to call up our friends and try to get them to come to an opportunity meeting, or at least read some information or watch a video about our MLM opportunity. To do anything different would be going against the number one commandment of our industry—duplicate what works. In other words, "Thou shalt not try to reinvent the wheel." I'm certainly not about to suggest otherwise. I do, however, believe there are very effective ways of making the wheel roll a little smoother and a little faster.

First and foremost, we must remember that when you propose your opportunity, you are offering a business opportunity. A chance at being a true entrepreneur. Second, you are proposing that your prospect get involved with multilevel marketing. In other words, you have at least one, and probably two, major challenges. Challenges you must overcome before you can even think about proposing your specific opportunity. Challenges that, nine times out of ten, are the main reason why your prospect won't even look at your opportunity.

Surveys indicate that about 85% of all working Americans would like to own their own businesses, if they could. In other words, if all obstacles were removed, they would prefer to be their own bosses rather than work for someone else. This amounts to approximately 200 million people! These are your MLM prospects. Now, when 200 million people want to do something and don't do it, there must be a good reason. When they are asked, they answer with the same four reasons every single time.

- It takes too much money. I don't have thousands of dollars to invest in a business.
- It takes too much time. I don't want to work eighty hours a week, seven days a week to get my business going.
- Too risky. More than 80% of all businesses fail in the first two years.
- I don't know how. I've never taken any business courses. I don't know anything about taxes, accounting, marketing, and so on.

I can assure you, if your prospects are not currently operating their own businesses, they have considered the possibility at some time in their lives. They have also determined all the reasons why they can't (probably all four reasons). Therefore, before you even start to offer your MLM opportunity, you might want to dispel, at least slightly, these beliefs about why they can't go into business for themselves.

Let's say you are having lunch with your friends and you casually mention the fact that you are thinking about starting your own business. Then you ask if they have ever considered it. Sure, they have considered it at some time or another. Well, why didn't you?, you ask. They will inevitably respond with one or more of the previous four reasons.

Now comes the fun part. You ask if they would ever consider going into business for themselves if the total start-up costs were under $500 and the income potential was higher than the earnings of some CEOs of Fortune 500 companies; if the total time investment could be as little as five to twenty hours a week; if they could continue to work in their present jobs until the income from their businesses is sufficient to earn at least an equal income and if they choose to discontinue their business they can return their inventory and marketing materials for as much as a 90% refund (try that with a franchise or conventional business), so there is little risk; and best of all, if there were numerous consultants available who are experts at running this business, who would train and advise them personally, for an unlimited number of hours, for the life of their business, absolutely free! Not only that, you say, but another company will take care of all your research and development, shipping, payroll, sales and payroll taxes, legal questions, and so on. And, this company will do this every month, for the life of their business, for about $20 a year.

Of course, your friend won't believe any of this. Ask your friends if they would consider it if all this were true. Most likely they'll say something like, "Well, sure. But there's got to be a catch." Is there? Isn't this an exact description of your basic MLM business opportunity? Is any of this even an exaggeration? No. You've just completed step A of the ABC Technique.

Now, for the first time during this conversation, you will suggest that this type of business involves "network" or "multilevel" marketing. But don't get into your specific opportunity yet. There still may be a major hurdle yet to overcome. You still have step B to take care of.

You are going to come across three basic types of people during your recruiting efforts. First, the cynic or skeptic. These people believe MLMs are all scams, get-rich-quick schemes, illegal pyramids, involve door-to-door and home-party sales, and so on. For whatever reason, these people have a low opinion of MLM in general. The second type don't know anything about MLM. Perhaps only that it's "something" like a pyramid, or that Amway or Shaklee are MLMs.

The third—unfortunately, smallest—group, are those who are naturally intrigued by the concept. Usually these people were originally in the second group, but heard about someone who made a lot of money doing MLM. By the way, if you find someone in this group, skip step B, which is presenting the MLM concept as a viable, honest form of business. This usually involves explaining what MLM is not, rather than what it is.

You may want to mention that more than six million people in the United States are pursuing this form of business. Mention that network marketing is a fifty-plus-year-old industry that includes more than six hundred companies. Also, throw out names like Rexall, MCI and US Sprint, Colgate-Palmolive, Gillette, Watkins, and Fuller Brush, which all have MLM divisions or resellers.

Briefly explain the obvious difference between an illegal pyramid and a legitimate MLM company, should this be a concern. In your information package, include favorable articles about the MLM industry in general. You may want to lead with a generic video or audiocassette that only legitimizes the industry, rather than promoting any particular opportunity.

Whatever you can do to give the industry more credibility, do it now.

Once these first two "preparation" steps are completed, you should then hand your prospect the video or literature about your specific opportunity. If your friends are still skeptical, challenge them to find the catch. Tell them you can't, even though you thought it was too good to be true also. Instead of trying to get them to find out what all the good things are about your program, encourage them to find all the bad things! Challenge them to debunk it. Let's face it. Someone would be much more likely to watch a video if it were for the purpose of justifying their negative beliefs, rather than contradicting them. It's human nature.

The bottom line is this: The real trick to successful recruiting in any MLM organization is not convincing someone who has looked at your opportunity to get involved with you, it's getting them to just look at the opportunity. Don't you agree? Let's face it, once someone seriously looks at a good MLM opportunity, it's pretty hard to not be at least a little intrigued. Unfortunately, nine out of ten won't seriously look. Actually, I'd guess five of ten won't look at all! You've got to get them to just look. If you've got a good opportunity, the rest will take care of itself.

A good analogy here would be the thermos and the VCR. Like the thermos, you must open your prospect's mind before you can pour anything into it. And like the VCR, you might have to remove something first. To borrow an analogy from Anthony Robbins (author of the *Personal Power* program), it's as if your beliefs have legs like a chair. Only these legs are usually solid steel instead of wood. Believe me, people's beliefs about why they can't go into business for themselves, and sometimes what they believe MLM to be, are solid beliefs. If you don't do something to at least weaken those legs before you come in with your new belief, forget it. It will bounce right off.

I'm certainly not suggesting that this ABC Technique is going to knock down those legs (although it could). But if you can at least instill some doubt in your prospect's mind, some spark of interest, or at least pessimistic curiosity, you've made a major gain.

I also realize this technique lends itself to certain situations better than others. For example, this technique might be a little more difficult to pull off if you do a lot of long-distance sponsoring. But it's still not impossible. Put it in writing, or better yet do your own audiotape (with company approval, of course).

For the last thirty or so years, in almost every MLM organization, we've all been taught to go straight to step C. Contact your prospect and propose your MLM business opportunity. "MLM" and "business" can be scary propositions, and needlessly so. Steps A and B are designed to reduce or eliminate this stigma, so you can bring more prospects to step C. Get them to just look!

Discussion

This article has appeared in seven MLM trade publications, including four that normally refuse previously published works. So I guess there's a lot of perceived value. Unfortunately, I still haven't seen this simple technique incorporated into any company training material. The focus still seems to be almost entirely on getting those who are looking to actually sign up, rather than getting more contacts to just look.

Let's say you contact one hundred prospects and ten actually take a good look at what you're offering. Of those ten, four sign up. So 40% of those who looked joined, but only 10% of those contacted looked. Wouldn't it then make more sense to try to increase the number of prospects you bring from step A to step B, rather than trying to improve the already successful process of recruiting those who are looking?

Figure 2.1 shows what would happen to your recruiting numbers if you could get 50% of those contacted to look, even if your actual closing rate of 40% never changed (compared with doubling your closing rate but never getting more than 10% to look).

Some might say you shouldn't waste your time on people who don't even want to look. Just say "next" and move on. To an extent I agree, but only in the most hopeless situations. Many, possibly most, of the most successful MLMers today

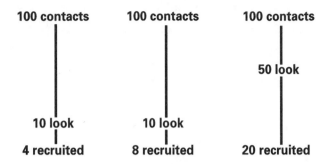

Figure 2.1 Increasing recruiting rate versus increasing looking rate.

likely resisted the concept of MLM when it was first proposed to them. I've heard story after story of people who claimed to have been extremely skeptical of MLM initially, only to have "seen the light" once they seriously considered it.

I firmly believe that the best network marketers in this country aren't involved in network marketing yet.

Why? They simply haven't looked close enough.

At the very least, bringing skeptics to the looking stage may not result in a total conversion, but it can dramatically reduce the number of skeptics breeding more skeptics. I think this would make all our jobs a little easier.

Gratuitous plug: Steps A and B of this technique are presented in my cassette tape, "Case Closed! The Whole Truth About Network Marketing." Check the end of this book for details.

* * *

In a way, I suppose it's a good thing that there is so much skepticism by "outer circle" folks, and that existing MLM distributors are so apprehensive about approaching them. As we'll discuss later, in half a century this industry hasn't even approached anything close to a saturation point. If every American were to ignore what they've been told to think, open their minds for a second, clearly and thoroughly evaluate network marketing without prejudice, and actually make their own decision, they'd probably all join!

But it doesn't take a downline organization of tens of thousands to be financially independent. I know many people who earn very comfortable livings with less than fifteen hundred in their groups. Keep in mind that the term "heavy hitter" is usually reserved for those with five thousand to fifty thousand or more distributors in their downline. So actually, you could be quite successful by sponsoring a single half hitter!

Where do you find these super networkers of tomorrow? How can you discover them before they've established themselves with another company? The mega-MLMers are all around you, right here, in . . .

The Land of 100,000 Unrecruited Heavy Hitters

Several months ago I received a call from one of my downline distributors inquiring about a good "MLM list." Bob then asked specifically if a list of "heavy hitters" existed and how I might approach them. My response was something to the effect of "Bob, why would you want a list of people who are the least likely to want to join your opportunity?" After all, heavy hitters are people who are making huge monthly incomes (that's why they call them heavy hitters, right?). I'd assume they like making huge monthly incomes and probably would not be too interested in walking away from it and starting over from scratch.

"But Len, think about it," Bob persisted. "Just imagine if I could have recruited . . ." Bob then reeled off the names of three major heavy hitters, all well known throughout the industry (we'll just call them Mark, Jim, and Ken). Bob began to fantasize about the great wealth to be had by recruiting the likes of even one of the three mega-earners he listed.

Well, I happen to know Mark, Jim, and Ken personally, to varying degrees, and I know their stories. Ironically, all these men claim to have once had a strong skepticism toward network marketing and at one time felt it was something they would never consider being involved in. Yet today, they are three of the richest, most successful network marketers in the country—as are their uplines!

"Exactly!" Bob exclaimed. "So how do we sign up people like that?"

Mark, Jim, and Ken were, at one time, not network marketers. Obviously. The lucky folks who personally sponsored these three did not do so by scrolling though existing heavy hitter lists. They worked hard on opening the minds of people who they thought had a lot of potential, got them to consider network marketing, and today they are set for life.

You see, about six million people are involved in MLM in this country today. About 285 million are not. This means there are literally thousands, perhaps tens of thousands of Marks, Jims, and Kens roaming around this country who, right now, are very skeptical of network marketing, who think they'll never be involved in it—who'll someday make somebody a million-dollar income! Thousands of them!

Personally, I think the very best network marketers are not involved in network marketing yet. Mark, Jim, and Ken are only the best out of the six million who are involved. The odds are that there are many people among the 285 million who are not network marketers who are far better network marketers then even Mark, Jim, and Ken are!

Today, we see a constant ebb and flow of distributors from company to company—those who migrate like Gypsies from program to program always looking for the better deal. And this segment of the MLM population is huge. The result is that many companies increase in sales volume and distributor count each month, but it's usually at the expense of another MLM program. Numerous companies that experienced growth in 1995 had that growth come primarily from the fallout of another MLM company.

Really, no company has experienced legitimate momentum in the last two years. Not like Herbalife in 1983, or NSA from 1987 to 1988, or NuSkin in 1991. Or, to a lesser extent, Quorum and

Melaleuca in 1992 and 1993. The point here is that these companies created this momentum by bringing in massive numbers of new distributors from outside the industry. And as a result, the industry grew as well.

But not today, at least not like in the 1980s and very early 1990s. Today, everybody seems to be into retreading existing distributors over and over and dreaming about landing the big heavy hitter. The industry has become sluggish and lazy, filled with a lot of spoiled opportunists looking for something for as close to nothing as possible. And the opportunities available to them have exploited and perpetuated this to no end. Where there was once an industry composed of merit-based opportunities that rewarded those who worked hard, retailed, and actually trained and supported their downline, there is now an industry full of fluff programs with token products that will basically sell you the farm for a small monthly personal purchase (certainly not all are like this—there are still many "traditional" opportunities as well, you just have to look a lot harder to find them). Again, the point is that recruiting "outer circle" people (those not involved in MLM) is hard work, and so few MLMers today are into working hard.

Why is it so hard? Because outer circle recruitment involves a two-, and usually three-phase process—and the first two steps are very tough ones.

Remember the ABC Technique? Step A is to open the prospects' minds to starting their own businesses. Even the idea of a simple "home-based" business might still conjure the four major dreads of most would-be entrepreneurs (too much money, too much time, too much risk, not enough knowledge, experience, or confidence). Step B is to overcome the concerns or apprehensions your prospects have toward network marketing in general. Step C is when you finally present your particular MLM opportunity—if you can get to step C. After all, steps A and B are really hard!

So, wouldn't it be so much easier to just find folks who are already involved in MLM, who've already gotten past these first two steps, and just convince them that your products are better and your compensation plan will pay them more? I mean, why go through all the trouble of taking them through steps A and B when someone else has already done the tough part for you?

Because—if you don't, this industry will not grow, your downline will be forever turning over as these transient MLMers move on to the next "better" deal, and—you will never recruit a heavy hitter!

There are thousands of them out there. Get out there and recruit one! Or recruit three!!!

Discussion

You might get the idea that everyone who is not involved in network marketing has some type of aversion toward it. Actually, I've found that most of the time step B is a snap simply because most people don't have any opinion about MLM at all. Many have yet to even hear about it! Again, I believe this is a result of participants within the industry only talking it up within the industry.

About two years ago I decided to travel across the country by train. I'd never been on a train, I was in no hurry to get to where I was going (to work in the home office of an MLM company) and the idea of having nothing to do for three days was a delightful one. During meals all the passengers sat in the dining car in groups of four. Rarely, if ever, do I recall sitting with the same person more than once. During these meals three questions would inevitably be asked of each person at the table: where are you from, where are you going, and what do you do?

Each time it was my turn to describe my occupation (I like to use the term "Professional Network Marketer") the response would be—every time—something to the effect of, "What's that?" And each time I described what I did in more detail, I was astounded to find that my dining partners didn't have a clue what I was talking about! Oh, sure, when I'd mention Amway or Mary Kay, there was usually some recognition of the name, but little more. And, keep in mind that most Amtrak passengers were older than fifty. These were no babes in the woods. They had lived long lives, gained a lot of knowledge, experienced many things—yet had no idea what network marketing was.

Pretty exciting, isn't it?

* * *

Another article I wrote about just getting prospects to look came after I had attended a seminar conducted by a Tony Robbins wannabe (much of his material came directly from Robbins' *Personal Power* tapes, in some cases verbatim) who was attempting to bestow the virtues of NLP (Neuro-Linguistic Programming) technology on a room full of MLM distributors. About the only thing he mentioned (this was an all-day event) that even remotely lent itself to building a successful downline, which was the premise of the presentation, involved discovering your prospects' "hot buttons." In other words, what is it they really want to hear that is specific to their personal agendas.

I had already been doing some research into this question, and it was already glaringly obvious to me that money was not the primary motivation of most MLM distributors or their prospects. At least, great wealth was not. It was always something else. This article addresses what most prospects want: how you can discover the real needs and desires of your prospects, and how to incorporate this vital information into the process of bringing more people to the looking stage.

What Do Your Prospects Really Want?

Everybody wants *money*, right? *Money, money, money!* Of course you know what your prospects want. What a stupid question. They all want more M-O-N-E-Y. How do you get them to join your multilevel opportunity? Why, just tell them how much *money* they'll make. Join our program and you could make *this much money*. Sure, there may be other reasons, but the main, primary, overriding motivation is always going to come back to the gobs of *money* you can make, right?

Wrong.

Think about this. If you had fifty thousand twenty-dollar bills in front of you right now (that's a million dollars), is it really what you want? It is? Then why would you go out and exchange all of it for something else? In other words, you would spend it. Because, it's not the *money* that people really want, it's all the stuff they can get with the money!

So the question you need to ask is, if my prospect had the money, what would he or she get with it? That's what your prospect really wants. Then proceed to explain how your opportunity can be the vehicle to acquire it. The end, not the means.

Granted, telling someone he or she could earn a million dollars with your opportunity can still be a fairly powerful, albeit misleading, motivator, but it's just so . . . cliché. Everybody says you can get rich in his or her program.

If you knew, for example, that your prospect wanted a bigger house, a new boat, and liked to fish, you could describe to him pulling up to the pier in the back of his huge, new home after an afternoon of fishing at his favorite lake. Of course, mention that he caught lots of fish.

If you knew someone who liked to ski and wanted a new car, don't tell her how much *money* she could make; tell her this could be a way she could drive to the mountains in her brand new BMW. Ski rack included.

What if your prospects are strangers, and you don't know these things about them? Just ask. Ask them simply: Why is it that you may be interested in getting involved in an opportunity like this? Don't assume anything. If their answer is vague, explore a little. Ask straight out, if you have to: What would you want out of this venture?

Naturally, they'll probably respond by saying they want to make *money*. But guess what. Of the more than one thousand people we surveyed, more than one-third didn't say *money*. As a matter of fact, they didn't mention any material gain at all! What they wanted was either "security" or "more free time." And when those who did say they wanted more money were asked why, about half responded with the same type of answer. More time, freedom, security, sense of accomplishment, recognition, and respect were common responses.

What all this boils down to is this: The majority of your prospects don't want more money, or even the material things it can be exchanged for, but rather the feelings they get by possessing money. When it comes to persuasion techniques, knowing what those feelings are can be an extremely powerful tool. And a dangerous one, if used unethically.

So you asked them what they want, and they said *money*. You asked them why, and they said they wanted more free time. If you can take this one step further and find out why they want more free time, then you've really got something to work with. Let's say they describe a situation where they feel they've neglected their families. They just don't spend enough time with their families like they should. Or, maybe they want to quit their jobs because they hate getting up so early and commuting for an hour. Describe, in vivid detail, how your opportunity could allow them to sleep in, work at home, be with their family, and so on, and you'll find many more prospects at least looking at your opportunity.

One last, but crucial, point. This can be powerful stuff. It should be used only for the purpose of getting your prospect to look at your offer. It should not be used to get them to actually sign up! This is not a closing technique. The final decision must be your prospect's, and it must be based on clear-headed, realistic expectations.

Notice how liberally we used the word "could" when suggesting the responses you might give your prospects. Suggest that your opportunity "could" provide them with whatever it is they're seeking. Don't imply that it "will" or even "should" solve their problems. Be realistic.

I am a very strong advocate of doing whatever it takes to get otherwise skeptical or disinterested prospects to at least consider MLM as a legitimate and worthwhile venture. This type of persuasion technique can be one way to help accomplish this. But don't defeat the purpose. Be sure you make clear to your prospects, at some point between looking and booking, that you are only offering the vehicle, they still have to drive it. And it's not an automatic!

Discussion

I recently spoke at a national kick-off for a new MLM company. I started my presentation by saying, "How many people here would like to learn how to make $250,000 per month, within six to eighteen months from today?" The response was less than enthusiastic. Oh, there was a smattering of applause, a few hoots and cheers, a couple hands raised, but mostly a lot of bad body language (furrowed brows, crossed arms). Someone even hissed and booed. I quickly explained to them that I was being facetious, and that this was not the type of ridiculous hype they were going to hear that afternoon. Those with their arms crossed relaxed. Those with their hands up sheepishly crossed their arms.

Later in that same presentation, I used one of the best "hot button" lines I've ever heard, at least for me personally. I asked them to imagine what it would feel like to wake up in the morning and absolutely know that all their bills will be paid this month whether they "roll out of bed—or roll over." This time I got a rousing ovation. They went nuts! These people were actually more excited about the idea of sleeping in in the morning than they were about making a quarter-million bucks a month!

I don't know who originated this ". . . or roll over" line, but I would like to thank that person. It's the line that moved me to get back into network marketing. And all of you who have ever called my office before 10:00 A.M. only to get my answering machine—now you know why.

Before we leave this subject, I do want to make one more comment about these persuasion techniques in relation to "selling" an MLM opportunity.

A couple of the persuasion techniques that I see taught at MLM training events involve what they call "mirroring and modeling." This is where you subtly mimic the mannerisms of your prospect. If they tap their feet a lot, you tap your foot a lot. If they like to hold pencils in one hand and scratch their heads with the other, you grab a pencil and start scratching your head. The result is that they will subconsciously create an attachment to you. They'll just like you more! After all, we all tend to be attracted to people who are like us, right?

Another similar technique involves watching your prospects' eye movements as they speak. If their eyes look up a lot, they're "visual" people. Side to side means they are "auditory" people. Down? That's "feeling" people. So if they tend to look up a lot, you're suppose to start peppering your conversation with visual connotations, such as "I see" or "Visualize if you will . . ." or "Take a look at this . . ." Again the result is that they will become more comfortable and feel closer to you.

Actually, this stuff works! I've tried it and it's almost scary what can happen. But the real question is this: Do you really want it to work with an MLM prospect? Maybe to move some product, sure. But remember that these are techniques that are being taught to recruit new distributors!

So let's say your prospect isn't really interested in your opportunity. So you start mirroring and modeling. You're tapping your foot, rubbing your nose. You start saying things like, "I really mean this from the *heart*, John. I really *feel* like you're *emotionally* ready for this *euphoric* opportunity!" Your prospect looks down a lot, you see. Suddenly, they just love you and everything you're telling them. They sign up. They go home, they wake up the next morning, call you up and say (as they're looking down, of course) "I'm just not that *excited* about this anymore. I *feel* like I've made the wrong decision." What are you going to do? Run over to their house, start rubbing your nose and tapping your foot, look down at the floor and tell them, "I don't understand your *feelings* about this, John. I'm really *depressed* that I didn't properly convey the *joy* of working this business. I would *love* for you to reconsider, and *feel* that . . ." Give me a break.

THE BEST PERSUASION TECHNIQUE IN THE WORLD IS A FAIR COMPENSATION PLAN, A SOLID, HONEST COMPANY, AND A QUALITY PRODUCT LINE.

It's a simple business, folks. You don't have to be a master persuader to succeed. Just get your prospect to look.

* * *

So . . . how do you close a prospect? That was the question I decided to deal with in the following article. In this case, I had just witnessed a top distributor for a major MLM company (he actually was pulling in almost a quarter-million dollars a month at the time) doing a training session at a local hotel. Part of the day was spent on closing techniques. They were the same stock closing lines they teach those telemarketers who try to sell you resort memberships or personalized pens. It was pretty pathetic to watch.

The Perfect Close

When it comes to the philosophy of MLM recruiting, the techniques and strategies are as wide and varied as the people involved in the industry. There are all kinds of suggested ways of finding a good company, locating leads, introducing your opportunity, getting people to opportunity meetings, conducting the formal presentation, and closing the prospect.

I believe that there really is no definitive right or wrong way of performing any of the latter steps in building your MLM organization. The success or failure of many of those "ways" depends, for the most part, on intangibles that only the individual distributor can determine. Who knows what's really the best way for Mary to cold call? Or, for John to conduct a presentation? Much depends on Mary and John's personalities, attitudes, motivation, communication skills, and the nature of their particular opportunities.

But when it comes to closing techniques, we really only advocate one method—across the board. It's a simple technique that will practically guarantee you an active, healthy downline, and a dramatically reduced attrition rate within your organization. And it's not that tough to pull off.

Enough suspense. When you've got your prospects at the stage of decision, when they've exhausted every last question, when it's time for the rubber to hit the road (when the pen hits the distributor application), and you're ready to spring that brilliant closing technique on them you learned at last weekend's training workshop . . . *don't!* Forget the "Double yes close," or the "Momentum close." Don't even think about trying the "Assumptive close." Try, instead, something brilliant like this: "So Cathy, are you ready to start?" Or perhaps something really clever like: "So, Frank, what do you think? Do you want to get started?" Or maybe even something a little bolder like: "Let's go for it! What do you say?"

I know you are probably thinking it must have taken me years of research and field testing to come up with such incredible closes. But seriously . . .

What I'm obviously saying here is, *don't* close them. The prospects must close themselves! Let me explain.

We must put this whole MLM recruitment game in perspective. Assuming the prospect is getting into this business to be successful, which would obviously be a safe assumption, then what are we really selling them here? No, not a used car, not life insurance, not a piece of real estate, but a livelihood! A means to earn a living. A way of life!

What is the true definition of a "close"? In my opinion, it is the artificial creation of, and inducement into, a decision. In other words, you did or said something that created a motivation, a feeling, that may not have been there naturally. If this is so, your new recruits will most likely go home, go to sleep, wake up the next morning and say, "Why did I do that?" And they'll have to be "closed" all over again. And again and again.

Even worse, you may have psychologically persuaded them into getting into something that they believed to be of more value to them personally than perhaps it really is. You may have closed them on the idea that your opportunity is something a little more than it really is, just to get them in. And a few weeks later, when they find out the truth, they can feel deceived or misled.

What we really need to look for are those people who will go home at night and can't sleep. Someone who will interrupt you near the end of your presentation and ask, "So how do I get started?" Even if you have to use one of the non-closes we offered earlier, you will at least leave it up to your prospects to make the final decision. And it will, hopefully, be their decision. Created naturally in their own minds, based solely on their own personal values, motives, and desires.

I do advocate doing whatever you can to get prospects to look at your opportunity (such as the ABC Technique). Looking never hurt anybody. But understand that getting them to look is completely different from getting them to sign up and actually pursue the business once they've looked. And, of course, you may have to eventually close the prospect on the idea of making a decision. Any decision . . . yes or no.

Sure, using this type of non-close can reduce your recruiting ratio a little. But what's the alternative? If you really want to just put people through the treadmill, get a few quick hits of product volume before they drop out, fine. Tell them whatever they want to hear. Just get their names on the dotted line. Throw the mud against the wall and see what sticks.

If, however, you're looking for some good, committed, serious people, let them show you who they are. You'll know when you find them. Sure, this can make your job a little harder. But nobody ever closed you by telling you this was going to be easy . . . did they?

Discussion

This article was actually kind of an ego buster. I thought I had some new and wonderful insight that the MLM world sorely needed to hear—only to discover that people like Tom "Big Al" Schreiter, Randy Gage, John Kalench, and many more had been advocating the non-close for years.

I guess great minds do think alike!

* * *

I made a point earlier in "The Perfect Close" that I like to expound on in my live seminars. There is no definitive right or wrong way of doing this business that applies to every distributor. Unfortunately, I've read quite a bit of material that suggests otherwise.

Take, for example, the issue of width versus depth. One very prominent networker and author advocates width pretty much universally (placing all your recruits on your first level). Another I know feels that depth is the only way to go (placing most of your recruits under each other). Well, how well do you think the width argument is going to fly with a distributor in a 2 × 12 matrix program (two wide, twelve levels deep), or a unilevel (no width limit) plan that pays 30% on level seven? Would you advise building deep in a break-away program that requires sixteen first-level, personally sponsored break-away groups to achieve the highest commissions?

What about the argument over which to lead with: the product or the opportunity? If your next door neighbor is speaking to you from over the hedge, and she says "You know, Jane, I'm thinking about starting a home business. I need some extra money," are you going to respond, "Who cares, Karen. Let me tell you about this great shampoo I'm using." Or, if she tells you, "My skin is so dry. I need to try a new brand of moisturizer," are you going say, "Life's a drag Karen. But I'll bet some extra money might cheer you up, huh?"

Okay, I'm exaggerating, a little. But do you see the point? There is no universal right or wrong answer to these debates. Personally, I'm a depth guy. But that's what works best for the program I work, those I work with, and my own agenda. Not having any idea what situation you're in, I wouldn't dare suggest that you should do what I do. The same with what to lead with. I believe you get investors with a company, customers with a product, and distributors with a comp plan—the fact that you need all three to be successful notwithstanding. These would just be my priorities depending on who I was talking to and their personal situations. Be flexible. Play it by ear. Once you get to talking with your prospect you'll know which approach to take.

One other common debate has been raging for years: When is the best time to get involved in an MLM opportunity? I addressed this issue at length in the month just before "The Perfect Close" article.

MLM Strategies—Ground Floor or Momentum?

One of the many controversies surrounding MLM "theory," is determining the optimum time to get involved with an opportunity. Pre-launch, ground floor, right before, or just after the momentum phase begins, after the company growth stabilizes, maturity . . . who knows for sure? There are pros and cons to getting involved in each stage of a company's growth.

First of all, forget "pre-launch." There's no such thing. Either you launched—or you didn't. Either you're accepting applications, moving product, and paying commissions—or you're not. The term "pre-launch" is a marketing gimmick to make the opportunity sound real "ground floor."

The major problem with getting involved with "ground floor" opportunities is that they are usually no more than one story high. Most start-up MLMs are long gone before the ink dries on their brochures. This failure rate seems to be dropping slightly amongst the more serious players in the MLM field, and it's not even close to the mythical "95% in the first eighteen months" claim, but even if it eventually matches that of conventional start-up businesses, it'll still be a risky proposition.

Another drawback to start-up operations is the lack of a sophisticated support base. When you try to go upline to get advice and support from those already successful in the business, and you reach the president of the company just two levels above you, where do you go? Few start-ups will provide video- and audiotapes, or at least good ones, right out of the chute. And how do you hold a convincing opportunity meeting with two people?

The flip side, of course, is that eventually you could end up at the tippy-top of a huge organization, *if* your company happens to become one of those that survive the long haul.

But even if the company does make it through that treacherous first year, you still may have to wait another year or two or three or four (or more) before any real substantial growth occurs. This stage is usually called the "momentum" phase, when name recognition starts to kick in and the geometric expansion of the organization really starts to explode. Well then, the best time to get in would be right before this momentum stage hits (it's just so obvious, isn't it?). Oh, and the best horse to bet on is the one that's going to come in first, the best stock to buy is the one that's about to go up, and the best person to marry is someone who's about to win $10 million in the lottery in a community property state. But, alas, this would all require a crystal ball, of course (or a good 1-900-psychic line).

When a company is about to go into momentum is totally speculative. Naturally, most young companies like to think, and will try to convince you, that they are on the brink of momentum. I've heard a company claim they were into momentum four days after they launched! In fact, I don't know of a single company that isn't going into momentum real soon.

Okay, so how about right after momentum hits? Some will say that's too late. That may even appear to be true, since a good indicator of when a company is in momentum is when everybody seems to be doing it. The saturation myth starts to take over. But if this logic were correct, then momentum would cease. Yet, momentum phases sometimes last many months, or even years. Some, though, are short lived and weak, and some never really occur at all.

And, by the way, this stage of an MLM company's growth cycle can also be crippling, or even fatal. Many times a company is not ready for it and can't keep up, and those that anticipate it may have to go into heavy debt since the revenues are not there yet (in fact, any company that claims to be "debt free" and "in momentum" is likely fibbing about one or the other). There is a big difference between an MLM company keeping up and catching up. It's usually the difference between life and death for the company. Once an MLM operation going into momentum gets even one month behind the growth curve, it's like letting go of the reins of a wild horse. Forget it. It's gone.

Keeping up means staying ahead of the growth curve. This means upgrading the computer system, adding more phone lines, hiring more employees, advance-ordering more inventory, perhaps moving to larger facilities, and all this usually occurs during the worst possible time—momentous growth! It's like changing a tire at sixty miles per hour. That's why it's not unusual to find companies using the term "momentum" and "growing pains" in the same presentation.

Let's discuss this momentum stuff in a bit more detail. This stage is actually a normal part of the growth cycle of any kind of business, only the upward curve of the graph tends to be much more acute, and the increase in sales more dramatic, in an MLM type operation because of the geometric expansion of the sales force.

I firmly believe that the whole MLM industry will someday go into a momentum phase. With more and more people wanting to work at home, or who are not working at all, this "alternative" form of income will become more and more intriguing. And with the technologies we have today that lend themselves to this business so well, such as fax machines, voice mail, conference calling, videos, satellite communication, the Internet, and so on, it will be an even easier (relatively) business to pursue. I think that this industry momentum will result in companies hitting their momentum sooner, and having the momentum last longer.

Not only do companies go into momentum, but individual downlines do as well. Eventually, if you stay with it long enough, this geometric progression will kick in for your specific downline. After all, it is just a mini version of a company downline.

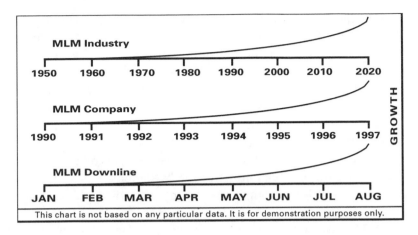

Figure 2.2 *Geometric progression (momentum) can occur within any size downline organization.*

Figure 2.2 reveals that this upward growth could occur at all three levels, to approximately the same degree. The only difference is that the industry growth is measured in decades, the company growth in years, and your personal organization growth in months.

So let's see . . . start-up is too risky and takes too long, pre-momentum is too speculative, post-momentum may be too late and can also be very risky—how about we just play it safe, be a little conservative, and get involved with a well established, middle-aged company that is just reaching its peak? Well . . . let's think about this.

There are basically three different stages, or tests, through which an MLM company must pass before it can really be considered "safe." One: start-up, which we've discussed. Two: momentum, which has its poisons as well. Three is the scrutiny phase. This phase usually occurs when a company is near its peak—when its distributor base is at its highest. This is also when their P-O total is at its highest!

A company's P-O factor represents the percentage of its total distributor base, both active and inactive, that are P-O'd!

Unfortunately, government regulatory agencies and the media don't go by the percentage, they go by raw totals. You could have a company with one million distributors and a 1% P-O factor, and another company with only one thousand distributors and a 90% P-O factor, and guess which one will get ripped in the media and attacked by attorney generals? The big guy. They've got ten thousand P-O'd people, whereas that little sleazy rip-off company only has nine hundred.

So getting in right at the peak, or just after momentum, can drop you right into the middle of the battlefield.

Some examples of companies that are victims of this test are United Sciences of America (deceased), FundAmerica (the Elvis of MLM, dead but there are still sightings), Herbalife (passed), Amway (passed), Mary Kay (passed), NuSkin (passed), American Gold Eagle (reincarnated into Gold Unlimited—which didn't pass), NSA (passed), Holiday Magic (long gone) and many, many more. Some who have made it through get set back and may have to face this stage again.

So what does this mean? Is it best to get involved with an old, mature company? Sure, it could work, but then you have to deal with the perception of saturation. And that's not counting the many hundreds of thousands of ex-distributors these older companies have racked up the last twenty or thirty years.

So what exactly are we saying here? *Never* get involved with an MLM company? Not at all. The real question you should ask is, What's best for you?

All phases of a company's growth have their advantages and disadvantages. Your risk factor increases the earlier you get in, but so does your income potential. You could label MLMers the same way you label investors. Conservative? Find a well-established company past the scrutiny stage. Aggressive? Go for "ground floor." Or, are you somewhere in between? Only you have the answer.

The bottom line is this: Any business venture has its risks. MLM included. Just pick the best opportunity for you, in a company that you feel comfortable with. Commit to it, work hard at it, and be honest and ethical at all times. If you and your organization can do these things, you will greatly increase your company's chances of being there for you in the long run.

Discussion

Width versus depth, product versus opportunity, and when to get involved are just a few of the "strategy" debates. There are many more.

Should you try to recruit long distance or only from your center of influence? There are so many factors involved in answering this one I won't begin to try to list them all. First, how much time and money do you have to invest? Long-distance sponsoring can get pretty costly. How many MLM programs have you been in before? In other words, do you have any center of influence left?

Personally, I'd go with the standard theory that your warmest contacts (best friends, family, and so on) are a terrible place to start. You'll probably spend most of your time listening to them try to talk you out of it rather than talking them into it. After you've achieved some degree of success is a much better time to approach these people. So, what degree of success have you reached? There are so many factors to consider. I'd be a fool to blindly tell you which recruiting approach to take without knowing you.

Should you inventory product? Should you hold opportunity meetings? Should you have home parties?

Yes—if you want to retail tons of products. But you know what? Tons of folks don't want to retail any products. They just want to personally consume their volume each month. I love doing meetings. Many MLMers today don't even want to attend them. But, many still do.

What type of plan should you join? Break-away? Binary? Unilevel or Matrix? Should the qualifications be high or low? Should the pay-out be strongest at the early stages of the plan, or should the commissions be loaded on the "back end?" All are good questions, and ones that no one can answer for you. It depends on what you're after.

Low-qualifying plans, or plans with the greatest pay-out on the first two or three levels, tend to spread the commissions around more. More earn a few hundred dollars per month, but no one ever gets rich. A high-qualifying, back-end heavy plan will increase your chances of becoming a millionaire, but there can be some long, hard, and very lean times along the way. No plan can completely satisfy both ends of the spectrum (I don't care how many say so). Which end would you be satisfied with? Or, are you somewhere in between?

Defining MLM strategy is like trying to generically define "business strategy" without even knowing what kind of business we're talking about.

Like any legitimate business, you should first lay out your objectives. You should create a business plan. After you are very clear about the various questions that have been posed here, and you know exactly what you are after, only then can you begin to define the strategy necessary to achieve those goals.

* * *

What do you do on a seven-hour flight to Orlando when you've already seen the movie and the person sitting next to you doesn't speak English? You sit and think. Being a 38-year-old, childless bachelor, it was only natural that I spend the first three hours thinking about my social life and raising a family (or more specifically, the dream of finally having the time to have one of each). Being a professional network marketer, it made sense that I'd spend the next three hours thinking about network marketing. Being a writer who had to come up with a column by Friday, I decided to spend the last hour thinking about both.

The result is as follows:

Courting MLM: Are We Ever Going to Get Married?

In many unfortunate ways, the correlation between human courtship and the way in which many of us "play the field" within MLM is disturbingly similar. In other ways, it is not similar enough. An analysis of how our species seeks out its mates compared with how we decide on which MLM opportunity to "commit" to might reveal a lot about the MLM condition in this country.

Let's take a look.

First, let's evaluate the four basic components of what we look for in a potential mate. First, there's physical appearance. Not just facial features and body characteristics, but style and dress as well. Second, there's personality. How easy is this person to get along with? How much does he or she have in common with your "world view"? Is he or she emotionally stable? How supportive and respectful a person is this? In general, how likable is this person? Third, at least in most cases, is the degree of this person's success. How much money does this person make? How much security does he or she offer? And the fourth and final consideration is that totally intangible, mysterious thing we call love. Which, by the way, most would agree has nothing whatsoever to do with items one through three.

So what are the basic components of what we look for in a good MLM opportunity? Well, I could answer that question by essentially reiterating the entire previous paragraph, making only a few minor word changes.

Certainly the overall appearance, or perception, we have of an MLM program is key. MLM is by far the most perception-oriented business opportunity is this country. Especially when it comes to compensation plans. Who cares what it really pays—how good does it look on paper? Right?

Does a company's "personality" make a difference? Ever been involved with or considered an MLM opportunity that didn't appreciate or respect its distributors? Was unstable? Had little in common with your philosophy or product interest? Just wasn't very likable?

Some folks may claim that level of success or amount of wealth is not a consideration when it comes to a mate (and most of them would be fibbing, at least to themselves), but it would be foolish to claim this makes no difference in picking an MLM program to commit to. It is a major consideration.

Even "love" comes into play.

I've found so little difference between the symptoms of love and infatuation, at least in the beginning. I've had crushes that I would swear were cases of true love. Only after years of experience and growth do we finally gain the maturity to tell the two apart (remember our grade school days when we were "in love" with every good-looking boy or girl in our class?).

Both infatuation (crush) and love can make us swoon, not eat or sleep for days, distract us, obsess us, make us act real goofy, temporarily enhance our efforts to look and act better than we normally do, and just get us all excited. The difference is that one stays and the other goes away! It's like two mountains. Time may weather away one mountain and turn it into nothing. There's nothing solid underneath to support it. Or, it could be like one of those volcanic mounds you see in Arizona landscapes where the loose, soft dirt washes away, but there's a strong, rock-solid core that will remain for centuries. In the beginning, from the outside, they both look pretty much the same.

Same with MLM opportunities.

Have you ever fallen in love with an MLM opportunity "at first sight"? Have you ever gone to a meeting or heard a presentation for the first time and left three feet in the air? Not been able to sleep that night? Got all excited and distracted? Has an MLM opportunity ever made you act at least a little goofy? (Be honest, now.)

Then, usually, it goes away, doesn't it? The novelty, the infatuation, the "crush" dissolves into nothing. And sometimes, usually after months or even years of searching, you find one that—oh, perhaps you lose a little passion for it after a while—you get comfortable with it. It works (always a good trait in a mate), it's supportive, it doesn't cheat, so you get complacent. And then, in those oh-so-rare and glorious, perhaps once-in-a-lifetime moments, you fall head over heels in love. And no power on earth will ever pry you away from that MLM program.

The comparisons are endless.

Ever fallen in love with an MLM program and then gotten dumped? Ouch! I swear it's the same kind of pain. It's awful. It eats you up inside thinking about the "possibilities," the lost promise, the fear of never finding another quite like that one.

Ever fallen in love with an MLM program and then settled down and had a family? You bet we have. That's exactly what MLM is all about, isn't it? In fact, both families and MLM downlines have something directly in common—it's called a genealogy!

Ever cheated on your MLM program by pursuing another one on the side? Or looked over another company's brochure and lusted in your heart?

Ever gotten overly protective of your MLM program? Trust me on this one—we have!

Ever created a lasting, fulfilling relationship with anyone while you were actively dating several others at the same time? Doubtful. Ever heard of anyone ever getting rich in MLM using the portfolio approach (several MLM programs at once)? Just as doubtful.

Think about the whole courtship ritual time line. Compare our agendas from the earliest moment of interest (in the opposite sex or an MLM opportunity) through to mature adulthood. The stereotypical, usually but not always male, junior-high-schooler was interested in "one thing." The immature, novice MLMer also seems to view his or her first MLM opportunity by not much more than how much it will "put out."

As we grew older, suddenly things like "good looks" and status came into play. We became at least a little more selective. We dreamed about "going steady," usually with the homecoming queen or the star of the football team (or both, if we lived in California). And as we gained more experience in MLM, we too found there was more to a good MLM relationship than simple lust (in this case for money). Suddenly, previously insignificant things like the product line began to take on more significance. The company's reputation mattered (because it affected our reputation as well). We became more selective.

Then, finally, we grew up. Stability and commitment became primary considerations. Oh, attractiveness still counted, but personality and compatibility became paramount. As many of you grizzled veterans of MLM would agree, there comes a time in your MLM career when the most important question about an MLM program becomes "will it last?"

In both life and MLM, there are, of course, variations to all of this depending on whether you're a man or a woman. But even those are comparable. For example, it's said that girls mature faster than boys. How many women do you know who are promoting or operating a money game or pyramid scheme? (In fact, the operators are almost exclusively men). It's said that women are more attracted by personality and other more emotional issues. Men are more interested in physical appearance. Again, is it any wonder that men are primarily responsible for the creation and promotion of MLM programs that simply "look good" with little or no substance behind them?

In some ways, it's too bad that we don't treat our pursuit of and commitment to MLM opportunities even more like we do our romantic relationships.

For example, how many people do you know who married the first person they were ever attracted to? Probably zero. How many people do you know who became a distributor for, and never considered any MLM program other than, the first one they were ever introduced to? I know many (including myself) who joined the first MLM program they were ever pitched on, then discovered there was a wide wonderful world of MLM opportunities to choose from—only to realize there were others they liked a lot better.

The divorce rate in the United States is now higher than 50%. From the glass half-full point of view, that means that 50% of all married couples stay married for the rest of their lives. Can you even imagine a network marketing industry where 50% of its distributors join one company and stay committed to it for life?!

Of course, one reason why some couples stay together is for the sake of the children. Have you ever stayed in an MLM program you didn't really care for anymore because you still had a downline?

Some couples with children do separate, usually followed by a bitter battle over custody. Do I even have to explain the correlation to MLM here? "Custody" battles over downlines and individual recruits are commonplace today.

Another reason why some married couples stay together, or perhaps why those that do divorce at least attempt to work things out, is that the divorce process (at least in most states) is an expensive, time consuming, pain in the butt. Even amicable, uncontested ones not involving children (trust me on this one, too). Also, there is a guilt factor for some as well. Remember, in most marriage ceremonies, we swore to God that, for better or worse, in sickness and in health (and so on and so on) we'd stay together ". . . until death do us part."

Here's Crazy Idea #247:

How about having the recruiting process involve, no, not a ceremony (unduplicatable), but at least some kind of written or verbal swearing in. Perhaps a signed (totally non-binding, non-legal) document in which the new recruit agrees to "marry" the opportunity, forsaking all others.

Also, make the divorce process tougher. If you had to go through some kind of elaborate, tedious, expensive process to leave your MLM opportunity to pursue another, perhaps we'd work a little harder on making our MLM marriages work.

Right now, the MLM industry seems to be mostly composed of adolescents who are being bombarded with "come-ons" from all directions. Is it any wonder there is so much promiscuity in this industry? Even those mature adults among us who have committed to a stable, loving relationship with an MLM opportunity are constantly being tempted by alluring competitors, and the money game sirens have driven more than one good MLM marriage onto the rocks.

Not only that, but bigamy and adultery are not only not illegal or immoral sins in network marketing—many of us openly encourage it!

(By the way, for those of you who just aren't getting it, I'm not saying MLM is full of bigamists and adulterers or that distributors practice promiscuity in the sexual sense. I'm making an analogy. MLM is full of people who fool around with more than one MLM program. Most of my readers are a pretty hip bunch and probably think I don't really need to explain this. But, trust me once again, someone is going to write me a letter or leave a voice-mail message telling me how offended he or she is for including them among adulterers and bigamists—even with this paragraph.)

Yes, there are times in both marriage and MLM that it just doesn't work. Even when you did all the right things for all the right reasons. Sure, MLM divorce is as inevitable and as justified as it sometimes is in married life. Occasionally, the MLM program we're in just isn't the one we fell in love with anymore. MLM programs change just like people do. Their values change. Their "appearance" changes. Their "personality" changes. And yes, sometimes they pass away.

But still, nobody today really gets married to their MLM opportunity. We're all just sort of "living with" our MLM programs. If we get mad at it, or things get a little bumpy, we just pack our bags and walk out the door. No big deal.

Perhaps it should be.

3

What We Should Not Be Doing (But Are)

I've long believed that success or failure in network marketing is not so much based on what we are doing wrong, but what we are not doing that's right! In other words, there are a lot more "right" things that we don't do than there are "wrong" things that we are doing. Thus the importance of the previous chapter. Nonetheless, so many people are doing so many things wrong that discussing it certainly can't hurt.

Possibly my biggest peeve of all, both in network marketing and life in general, are people who don't take responsibility for their own actions (or inactions). People are always blaming someone or something else for their failures. Failed MLM distributors is a classic example. Every single thing these distributors did or didn't do that caused them to fail was a direct result of a decision that they made voluntarily, of their own free wills.

Think about that. Name one situation where a failure could be completely beyond the direct control of the distributor. I bet right now there are thousands (hopefully) of readers thinking "a failed company?" What is an MLM company? It's a shipper and supplier of product and an administrator of your organization. If this organization goes out of business, find another one! Of course, keeping your organization intact can be a challenge, especially if you pick several losers in a row. Even then, it's an excuse for a setback, but not for complete failure.

Even if you lose your entire downline, there are a few million other people out there, and a few hundred other companies. In fact, I know very few successful distributors who are still with their first MLM program. Most have been through several (one after the other) before finding a home. I've been through seven in seventeen years (four in the first three years).

The real catalyst to this next article was an article I read in the *San Francisco Chronicle* in October 1991. The article featured a picture of two fiftyish looking men with real sour expressions on their faces. They were P-O'd. They were professional businessmen who had been duped into buying $5,000 worth of water purifiers. They could only sell two or three and were now forced to dump the purifiers at half their cost just to recoup at least some of their losses. These men were, of course, suing the company. They had been scammed.

One of my clients in the computer business I owned at the time, who was also a personal friend, got involved with this same company about the same time. My friend wisely bought only $1,000 worth of both air and water purifiers, and sold them all! My friend was not a professional businessman or salesperson, like the two gentlemen in the picture. She was a twenty-three-year-old, junior-college student living in the Mission District of downtown San Francisco!

Staring at that picture of those two men staring back at me with those angry scowls just burned me up inside. Although the following article was written several months later, when I was in a more peaceful state of mind, I never forgot my friend and that picture.

MLM Failures: Who's Really Responsible?

I was recently asked at one of my Facts & Myths of MLM seminars what I thought were the top five reasons for people failing in MLM. When I opened that question up to the group, I heard, again and again, stories about those who were front-end loaded, who had to stockpile tons of product to meet quotas, who were misled or deceived into believing in a worthless product or opportunity, duped into believing there was little or no work involved, or simply got involved with a failed company.

Not one time during this rather lengthy exchange did anyone suggest that perhaps the individual distributor was at
fault. The company, the sponsor, the products, the compensation plan, or the MLM concept was always to blame.

In no particular order, here is a list of what I've found to be
the top five reasons for distributor failures. Take note, as you
make your way through each point, who is really responsible.

Lack of Knowledge

Many people just don't seem to take their business seriously.
Heck, most won't even acknowledge it as a business. It's
just this plaything they take out once in a while to try to get
rich with. Then, of course, they toss it in the dump when it
doesn't perform.

Any legitimate MLM opportunity is a business opportunity,
no less genuine than any other. But this type of free enterprise
isn't taught in school. No, not in Harvard, or Stanford, or anywhere else (nor will any major college or university ever offer
a course in any profession that does not require a college
degree). You have to learn how to do it, and this education
process, although not usually long or complicated, is still
worthy of much more than a quick flip through your distributor manual.

If you want to make a comfortable living out of MLM, you
must go to school. Read MLM books (there are many good,
generic books), listen to tapes, go to training meetings, read as
many of the MLM publications as you can, and learn everything there is to know about your product line or service. Call
up your upline and ask questions. Do your homework first!

The Junkie Syndrome

There is no basis for this figure, but I would guess that less than
10% of all MLM distributors who have been actively pursuing
this business for more than one year are still with their first
company. Most have been with several. Of course, this is not

always the sign of a junkie. I personally have been involved with several, but they kept going out of business (this was years ago, when I didn't do my homework).

I believe MLM junkies fall into two categories. First, there are those that believe, "If I can make $1,000 doing one program, I can make $10,000 doing ten!" These are the folks who are distributors in ten programs simultaneously. Then there are those who believe that the cash is always greener on the other side of the fence. These people are in whatever program was presented at the last opportunity meeting they attended. They're in ten companies in ten months.

I know a gentleman who used to brag about his "expertise" regarding the MLM industry. He was quite proud of the fact he had been involved with twenty-one companies over the last fifteen years. Of course, he hadn't made any money in any of them, but the one he'd just signed up for was going to make him rich! Again.

Pumping Up the Volume

By this, I'm referring to the act of artificially meeting group and personal volume quotas by stockpiling product with money out of your own pocket. This also includes the act of front-end loading your new recruits.

From all the feedback I get from the field, and from all the press MLM receives, it seems obvious that this is a major killer of MLM success, not only for the recruits who are victims of this practice, but for the experienced distributors as well. And in some cases, even the company itself is ruined by it.

Last year, while investigating a company for a future review in *MarketWave,* I went to an opportunity meeting and later met with one of the representatives. She strongly encouraged me to sign up for $500 worth of product because that was this program's personal monthly volume requirement for advancement. Of course, I also needed $2,000 monthly group volume, and five active front-line distributors . . . and it was the 25th of the month! But that wasn't discussed.

There was absolutely no excuse for her to suggest that kind of purchase, other than to increase her bonus check. By doing this, she runs the risk of either blowing out her prospect's budget the first month, turning the prospect off completely, or losing the prospect's trust and credibility not only in her but also in her company. And besides, front-end loading is illegal! Sure, this company didn't require a product purchase at start up, but these people were actually being taught by their upline to not sign anyone up unless that prospect bought at least $250 in product. Otherwise, their downline would be "poisoned."

I agree new distributors should buy some amount of product, but at a time and amount they are comfortable with. Which would you rather have, a distributor do $1,000 in volume and quit in a month or two, or $100 in volume for the rest of his or her life?

What I think is even worse than front-end loading, as far as cause for failure, is stockpiling. There are so many people who are either over-anxious, lazy, desperate, or just plain ignorant when it comes to this practice. They think if they take money out of their own pocket and meet all the monthly volume quotas, they won't have to retail, or perhaps they'll sell it all later. Or, they may not want to wait to naturally meet the criteria for higher bonuses by building a retail base or downline so they buy in at some huge amount of inventory. Of course, sometimes they do this out of desperation. Their downline is dwindling fast, or maybe they had a lot of people break away all at once.

This might be a fair excuse for a month or two, maybe. But I've heard of people who stockpile every month. I used to know a guy in a popular break-away program who purchased $3,000 worth of product one month to maintain his status level, because all his eight front-line people broke away. He claims to have quit this business with over $5,000 worth of product rotting in his garage. Here's a thought. Do whatever you did to get eight front-line break-aways and build your front line back up. Okay, maybe he couldn't wait. Maybe he quit his job to do this full time, and couldn't afford the lower bonuses in the meantime.

My suggestion? Don't quit your job until your status is secured. I'm not trying to be sarcastic here, I'm simply trying to suggest that these situations all stem from bad business decisions on the part of the individual distributors.

Another motivation for loading and stockpiling probably comes from the idea that MLM is a get-rich-quick or get-rich-easy scheme. When naive distributors discover they actually have to work to make MLM work, they try to circumvent the rules. They attempt to make it a get-rich-quick-and-easy scheme anyway. Some less reputable companies even try to design their programs to meet this end. It never works in the long run.

The worst thing about this practice is that once the disgruntled distributors give up and quit with this mountain of accumulated stock, they bad-mouth the company, their sponsors, and the industry in general. They file class action suits, go on TV, get interviewed by national magazines . . . and every MLM distributor suffers because of it.

Distributor Apathy

Probably the most obvious reason for failure, in anything, is simple lack of action. Especially in MLM. So many distributors are convinced that to be successful in this industry you get other people to sell for you. And in many programs, they even believe their upline will build their downline for them as well. And, of course, some distributors are just not very motivated or are just plain lazy. They want all those wonderful benefits they heard could be achieved in MLM, but they don't want to do what is necessary to achieve them.

The more a company, or its distributors, continues to promote its opportunities as ones that require little work, or that can provide success "easily," the more it is going to attract people who don't want to work, who are going to take it easy. And when they fill their downline with these people, they wonder why nothing happens.

During my seminars, I like to tell the story of a man who is looking for a chisel (an MLM opportunity). A tool he can use to carve out a sculpture (carve out a living). He does his home-work. He shops around and looks over several chisels. After studying each one thoroughly, he excitedly makes the purchase (signs up). Then, he goes home and puts the chisel away. Days go by. The block of wood stands ready, but untouched.

Occasionally, the man takes the chisel out and ponders it. Fantasizes about what he could create with it. He keeps hearing great things about this brand of chisel. It's sharp, straight, and accurate. Very comfortable to hold. Once in a while, he takes a stab at it, literally. Makes a few scratches here and there. A few shavings fall to the floor. Weeks go by. The block of wood is still shapeless. Spider webs begin to form at its base.

The man begins to notice what little effect this chisel has had on his carving. It's just not taking shape, he says. Damn chisel! I've been had, he thinks. My family was right all along . . . these chisels are nothing but junk! They never work. Not just this brand, but all chisels, he assumes. He throws the chisel into the trash. Then, at work the next day his co-workers ask him how his carving is doing. Terrible, he says. Those chisels are nothing but junk. Don't ever buy any of them. It's not my fault. I don't have the right tools. But I'm going to the hardware store tomorrow—I'll find something that works!

I Quit!

MLM is the one form of business where you could accurately state, "If you fail long enough, you will succeed." I've heard many times that in MLM you cannot fail, you can only quit. I believe this is accurate.

I met a woman after a seminar one night who informed me that she was going to quit her opportunity because, after four months at it, she was "failing miserably." I asked her what that meant in numbers. She replied that she had signed up "only" two people her first month, none the second and third, and two more her fourth month. Four in four months. I then explained to her that if she were to continue to "fail miserably" for eight more months, and each of the people she sponsored were to fail just as miserably as her, at the end of the first year a grand total of 4,096 people would have joined her downline. If only one-fourth of them were active to any degree, she'd still be earning a few thousand dollars per month. If only we could all fail as miserably!

Of course, math is perfect and the real world is not. I made it clear to her (as I am to you) that such a progression is actually quite optimistic and unlikely. Still, the point was this: the more people who join your downline, the more people are helping you build it! Of course the progress will be slow at first; only one person is doing the building—you. But sign up just one person and you've doubled that number. If that person sponsors just one, and you sponsor another, you've doubled the number again. There are now four times as many people all working to build your downline. Based on the 1×1 progression, you would only have had fifteen in your group after the fourth month and would probably be earning less than $100.

Yes, it's tough to stick with it when everyone is telling you how you'd be rich by now in their deal. But take a look at where you are going. Take whatever success you have had and project it out over a few more months, or even years. The finish line is there, but you'll never reach it by running back to the starting line. Every time you quit, you kill the progression and start over at one again.

Sadly, thousands of folks are doing just that, every single day. And they're all wondering why they can't succeed in network marketing.

Notice where the responsibility lies within each of the above points. Not with the company, or its products, or its marketing plan, or even its distributor base. It falls on the distributor alone.

SO MANY DISTRIBUTORS WORK THE BUSINESS WRONG, THEN CLAIM THE BUSINESS IS WRONG WHEN IT DOESN'T WORK!

Yes, yes, the company could go under. But if you've done your homework, the chances are increased that even this dreaded scenario could be avoided. And if it does, it will only be a setback, not an end to your MLM career.

What about the guy who quit his job, bought $5,000 worth of water purifiers, sold one to his mom, and then joined a class-action suit against the company? He was deceived. Lied to. Scammed! It wasn't his fault . . . was it? No—if someone held a gun to his head and forced him into it. Otherwise . . .

I hear about this kind of thing happening all the time. Some distributors make very emotional, uneducated, terrible business decisions, then look for a scapegoat.

Let's say you owned a video rental store and a supplier offered you a great deal on one thousand copies of *Ishtar,* which you agreed to sight-unseen. Later you found that only one was rented. Would you sue the supplier you bought them from? Sure, some would. But who could have read reviews of the movie, called other video stores to see how well *Ishtar* was moving, bought one and tested it first, or just watched the movie? Who's really responsible?

In today's information age, especially with the abundance of information sources available in and to the MLM industry, there is absolutely no excuse for a new distributor to go into an MLM opportunity unaware of the truth. A few simple questions, a couple phone calls, and a little bit of reading is all someone needs to do to know exactly what will really be expected of them, and what to expect from MLM, to be successful.

Multilevel marketing works! The concept is sound, and the good, legitimate opportunities are everywhere. Everything you will ever need to succeed in this industry is out there, right now. The only ingredients still to be added to the mix are hard work, patience, knowledge, honesty, and commitment. Things we must provide. All of us. We are responsible!

Discussion

I want to expound a bit on this issue of lack of knowledge. I want to make it clear that MLM is basically a simple business to operate. Not easy, but simple. It doesn't take a lot of business or marketing knowledge to be successful at it. That's one of the beauties of it.

It's not so much a lack of knowledge, per se, as a naiveté, or lack of MLM savvy. Once you have it, you gain a sophistication that allows you to see through a lot of the empty promises and hype-filled pitches that many (but not all) of the programs use to entice you.

Let's take downline building services as an example. Suppose you saw an ad that "guaranteed" this service would place at least five others in your downline within thirty days, for a fee of only $25. How can this work? Why, by making the same offer to five others, of course. How could these others refuse a deal like that? Of course, twenty-five more will have to accept the offer to keep those five happy. And 125 more to satisfy the guarantee to those twenty-five. And—I'm sure you saw this coming—by the seventh month the service needs 78,125 more who will believe their promise of five more to each of them.

Incidentally, this type of scam pops up several times a year and usually lasts about four or five months before the math blows up in the face of the perpetrator. In the meantime, however, he's managed to get a few thousand prospects to pay him to join his downline! What a deal—for the guy at the top.

By the way, I'm using masculine pronouns here deliberately. I've never found a downline building scheme operated by a woman. Not one.

A more clever way of guaranteeing a downline is the ol' reverse matrix scam. This is where a downline-building service places about one thousand very gullible, or at least very trusting, individuals into usually a 2 × 9 matrix (two wide, nine levels deep). After it fills, the perpetrator tells you, everyone will be reentered into another 2 × 9 matrix in reverse order! Those at the top of the first one will make about $5,000. If you're at the bottom, don't worry. You'll be at the top of the second and also make $5,000. If you're in the middle, then you'll end up in the middle of both and make $2,500 from each. Amazing! How can you lose?

Easy. The bottom level of the first matrix holds 512 people. Exactly how can 512 people be placed into the two positions at the top of the next matrix? Remember this little mathematical rule: In any matrix that progresses 2×2, any level will only hold two more than all previous levels combined. So, that means that levels one through eight will only hold 510. Not only will 256 of those bottom 512 end up on level eight (second from the bottom) of the second matrix, but a real unlucky two will end up on the bottom level of both!

Or, how about this deal? All you do is "pledge" or "promise" to sign up and buy product in a company only after the downline-building scheme has received one hundred pledges after you. Notice there is usually no guarantee that any of those one hundred will actually go into your downline. And even if there were, guess how big your organization will be once it happens? That's right. Zero. You will have one hundred people who have promised they will join your downline as soon as another hundred are found to place under them. And so on, and so on . . .

Here's a downline-building scheme (originally exposed by Tom Schreiter in *Fortune Now*) that, quite frankly, I think is ingenious, at least in how it makes the operator money. The offer is made to build your downline for you in exchange for, say, a $1,000 "promotional fee." This money will be used only to cover the expense of advertising, phone bills, direct mail pieces, and all the other expenses involved in building your downline for you. All you have to agree to is a minimum product purchase each month to qualify for your check. The kicker is that if after one year the promoter of the scheme has not gotten your monthly income to at least $1,000, he guarantees to refund the difference between what you are earning and your initial $1,000 fee. If you are earning nothing, you get your entire grand back. Assuming he will actually live up to his guarantee, this is another "can't lose" offer, right? Let's take a look "inside."

Let's say one thousand people go (fall) for it (not an unrealistic number, sad to say—I've seen downline-building schemes bring in four to eight thousand participants). So the operator, let's call him Sam, has $1 million in the bank. Invest that in CDs or mortgages at 9% interest and Sam's made a cool $90,000 in interest—and he's got the whole million left at the end of the year to live up to his guarantee! Not only that, but the monthly product orders those one thousand people make each month would easily generate $50,000 in volume, earning Sam another $3,500 each month in overrides!

But wait, there's more. Many of those at the top of this thousand-person downline are going to earn commissions from the volume generated by all those below them who are ordering their monthly minimum. Let's say two hundred of them average $200 in earnings per month at year's end. That's $40,000 Sam doesn't have to refund! Some distributors will not make their monthly order or will drop out, voiding the guarantee. Some will recruit and build on their own. Many who are earning $500 or more each month won't even ask for the guarantee. Sam could easily net over $150,000 free and clear after fulfilling his guarantee, and not do one single thing to build the downline!

(Lord, why did you give me a conscience?)

Another example of a lack of MLM savvy (or "Street Smarts" as Robert Butwin calls it in his book) is this idea that pursuing several programs simultaneously puts you at some kind of financial advantage. Our studies have shown that 51% of all network marketers in the United States are pursuing just one MLM opportunity right now. The dual approach is being tried by 29% of them, and 12% are operating three at the same time. So we could safely say that there is a definite lack of MLM savvy among most of the remaining 8% who are actually trying to promote four or more opportunities at once. The record, from just my own experience, for most MLM programs pursued in a lifetime is thirty-six. Most at one time is eighteen! And both of these folks are still trying to find the "right" opportunity for them.

Do you know how to tell when a company is having financial troubles, or is just getting greedy? There are signals you can watch for that are a real tip off, but hardly ever noticed.

This usually involves a cut in commissions, but some companies even manage to make the reduction appear to be a generous enhancement to the compensation plan.

For example, any time a company shifts commissions from the front-end of the plan (the early stages where most new distributors are) to the back-end (where the few highest earners are), it will create the opportunity for more income potential and make income projections on paper look even better. Actually though, this would result in a drop in overall commission expense because the weakened first few stages of the plan are where most of the distributors are.

I know of one fairly prominent company that added a whole new seventh level onto its plan, thus allowing another huge step of exponential growth (at least on paper). No other major change was made to the plan itself. What many excited distributors didn't notice, at least until they received their next checks, was that the basis for determining commissions was also changed from retail amounts to wholesale—and checks actually dropped as much as 30%.

Another company claims it will pay you twice, based on two different kinds of compensation plans, on the same group sales volume. One plan overlays the other. What you soon discover (usually after joining and getting your distributor kit) is that each product is assigned a point value, called Bonus Value, which is the basis for computing commissions—and the Bonus Value of each product averages about 56% of the wholesale price. Sure, you are paid on two compensation plans, but only on about half the volume!

But let's not dwell on the negative. Actually, many companies are shifting commissions the other way—from the back to the front. Some are just flat out adding more bonuses. There seems to be a trend right now toward reducing qualifications and quotas (in some cases to a fault), which will make income levels more achievable. Overall, the industry is slowly getting more and more generous!

* * *

The best way to gain knowledge, to gain MLM savvy, is to ask questions. Why, when, how, who . . . But there's kind of a catch-22 here because you already need a little MLM savvy to be able to ask the right questions.

A perfect example would be the questions we ask in our attempt to discover if an MLM program is really a pyramid scheme in disguise. It's great that so many of us are asking that question now, and I've been so pleased lately to see the diligence many new distributors are taking in their initial investigations into potential opportunities. But again, it's not so much how many questions you ask, it's what you ask and how you ask it that counts.

Regarding this pyramid question, here's an article I wrote just as a sidebar in a recent issue of *MarketWave*.

Is This a Pyramid Scheme?

"Questionable" MLM programs continue to flood the market at a record pace. But unlike their predecessors, they're hiding their true natures better than ever. Many quasi-pyramids and money games today are taking great advantage of the ignorance of most people about what constitutes an illegal pyramid. Please understand, I do not use the term "ignorance" derogatorily. The term comes from the word "ignore" and many of us are simply ignoring two basic, simple facts that make up a composite of a typical pyramid scheme. Also, understand that I am not an attorney, an attorney general, or a postal inspector. But I know what questions they ask—and so should you!

One of the most common, and least accurate, questions we're taught to ask is, "Is there a product involved?" Terrible question. Almost every pyramid out there today has thrown in some kind of token product knowing you'll ask that question. Some extremists will go so far as to tell us that the "service" they provide in exchange for your fee is their administration of the intake and outgo of cash. Some will claim you are paying to have your name added to a mailing list! Of course, the typical chain letter leads you to believe you are paying for a report of some kind. There are literally dozens of schemes, however, that are not nearly as obvious. Some offer what appears to be an abundance of bona fide, tangible products.

One of the best examples I can recall was a program called The Ultimate Money Machine. For $300 you were to receive such items as luggage, a 35mm camera, and a seminar on cassette tape valued at, of course, hundreds of dollars. Well, the camera was a cheap, plastic job that *Sports Illustrated* couldn't give away, and the luggage you unrolled from a tube. Total cost to the company for all of these products was probably less than ten bucks!

A program called Euro-Round required a $100 payment in exchange for nothing. Later, to "make the program legal," Euro-Round added a little book.

Remember Marathon? Here you were asked to invest over $2,000 for a series of cassette tapes and some literature. The participants claimed that "education was priceless." Let's give them the benefit of the doubt and say the information may even have been worth the $2,000. I guess it's possible. Unfortunately, this was an ongoing monthly fee! Were the tapes and literature supplied by Marathon worth over $24,000 to a participant who'd been in for a year? Probably not.

Several companies today offer product vouchers or certificates that can be spent on items out of a catalog or from various local merchants. They then claim to be offering "thousands" of products. Uh uh. They are only offering the funds to purchase these products from third-party, unrelated vendors. How many folks do you know who would be willing to purchase a $200 product certificate for $200 cash?

So don't just ask if there is a product involved. Question whether the product is even close to being worth the overall price paid. You don't have to be an economics genius to know the answer. Just ask yourself this question:

WOULD ANYONE REALISTICALLY EVER PURCHASE THIS PRODUCT OR SERVICE WITHOUT PARTICIPATING IN THE INCOME OPPORTUNITY?

Thousands of people purchase products from such companies as NuSkin, Watkins, Herbalife, and Amway every day without becoming distributors. They just want the product. This is true for most of the MLM companies out there. But ask yourself, "Would anyone have ever subscribed to *Washington Power Digest* for $125 per year just for the publication alone?" Very few. Did many people pay over $350 to Consumer's Buyline just for the $39 discount buyers service? Doubtful. How many folks would pay more than $30,000 for a two-day seminar in the Bahamas, as was offered by CommonWealth and several other such schemes? Unless it was one helluva seminar, probably no one.

Another consideration is whether or not there is any kind of financial reward for just the act of recruiting. But this question is trickier than it seems as well.

For example, what if a product-based company also offered upline commissions on sales aids and training fees? Wouldn't it then be possible to earn commissions by just signing up new distributors and getting them trained and ready to do the business of selling the products—long before they've actually sold any products?

The key question here is, Does the product or service have value to someone who just wants the product or service? Is it retailable? Again, would someone pay for it even if this person was not a distributor? So, would someone go to your company's distributor training meeting or buy your company's brochure if he or she were not going to participate as a distributor? Of course not.

Does the company claim you only have to make a one-time purchase? I've seen several programs recently that claim you pay once, then sit back and wait for the residual income to roll in. But think about that. Where is the "new" money coming from? Obviously a company can't pay out more than it takes in, so the only way the program can continue is if people keep recruiting.

So, even if the "one-time" fee is for a perfectly legitimate, tangible product of reasonable value, and upline commissions are only coming from that purchase, it may still violate the principle of a financial reward for the act of recruiting.

If you're not convinced, then ask yourself this question:

"IF ALL RECRUITING STOPPED TODAY, WOULD THIS COM-
PANY STILL BE ABLE TO PAY MONTHLY COMMISSIONS IN THE
MONTHS AHEAD?"

If you only have to pay a one-time fee in the beginning, then
the answer would be a definite *no*. Eventually all the existing
funds would be used up and no new funds would be coming
in. Commissions could only be paid if people continued to
recruit. Whereas legitimate, legally sound MLM companies
could continue to pay commissions from the ongoing buying
and selling of their products.

So if you can't answer the above two questions with a confident, resounding "Yes," you should probably tell your prospective sponsor "No!"

Discussion

I want to make it clear that the previous article is not necessarily based on the author's opinion of the way it should be. It's
simply the way it is. Personally, I believe we are all intelligent,
mature adults and should be allowed to do whatever we want
with our own money as long as there is full disclosure and we
are made aware of the risks involved. Also, much of this discussion is based on years of precedent, not just my layman's
interpretation of the law.

In fact, the roots of most MLM law is founded on the
Amway v. FTC decision in 1979. Perhaps the single most defining characteristic of a legal network marketing company came
from these hearings. Essentially, the question was asked . . .

CAN THE LAST PERSON IN STILL MAKE MONEY?

Obviously, the last person in a pyramid scheme (the most
obvious of which have no product at all, only a cash investment) will never make a dime. But if you were the very last
person to ever sign up as a distributor for Amway, NuSkin, or

Shaklee, could you still make money? Of course. By buying the product at wholesale and selling it at retail. In some MLM compensation plans it would even be possible to earn commissions or bonuses based on national bonus pools, car allowances, or other prize awards.

If you were the last person to sign up in your MLM program, could you reasonably expect to be able to mark up the product or service and resell it to an end user? That is, someone who only wants the product or service.

Understand that I'm not suggesting that any company that might be violating any of the previous three principles is necessarily going to be shut down. First, federal and state regulators don't go out searching for them. Usually, someone must bring these companies to the attention of the regulators. As long as the scheme is keeping people happy and no one complains, it could last for years.

There are also some very good, honest programs that might not receive a "yes" answer to one or more of these questions. For example, I know of one very promising program that does pay commissions on sales aids. Again, that does not necessarily put the program in dire jeopardy. If a regulator has a problem with this, the program will just stop paying commissions on sales aids. Most of the time, unless it's just an outright scam, the offending company will be given the opportunity to fix the problem long before there are any serious consequences.

* * *

One of the most basic concepts of MLM is to learn from the success of your upline. Find someone who has made the program work and duplicate what he or she did. Of course, this same idea can be put to good use if applied in reverse. Find people who have failed and don't do what they did.

Specific types of MLM programs have been around for many years that simply never work. But unless you've been around the industry for many years, you may not be aware of this. Experience is by far the best teacher, and that's where you'll gain most of your MLM savvy.

For those who don't have the benefit of years of MLM exploration, here are four examples of what I mean.

MLM Programs That Never Work—But Won't Go Away!

A psychiatrist friend of mine (just a friend, I swear), once told me that the clinical definition of insanity was the act of doing the same thing over and over and expecting different results. For example, if you stuck your hand in the middle of a campfire, you'd likely not do it again. If you did, and got burned once more, you'd probably have to be a little nuts. For sure if you tried it a third time.

So how many times do network marketers have to get burned before we realize what's safe and what's dangerous?

In their defense, I find it rather rare that the same person subjects himself to the same doomed-to-fail type of MLM program over and over. In fact, it is usually a case of once burned and good-bye (unfortunately, it's usually good-bye to the entire industry). But think about it. If you were sitting around a campfire with five other people and each of them placed their hand in the fire and got burned, isn't it about as nuts for you to follow them? How many times do we have to watch other people get burned before we get the picture?

But that's not really fair. (I love having arguments with myself.) Most network marketers who subject themselves to doomed-to-fail type MLM programs are usually new to network marketing. Let's face it. The swift turnover rate in this industry also causes it to have a very short memory.

Fine. So for all you "new" folks out there, here is a brief list of fires to not stick your hand into.

Gold and Silver Programs

This one is number one on the list for a reason. This has got to be the most "doomed-to-fail" type of MLM program that has ever existed. Since I've been involved with MLM (about seventeen years) I've seen dozens and dozens of Gold and Silver programs start up—and go away. Over and over and over. And usually for the exact same reasons.

Over and over and over.

There are three primary reasons why these programs fail and why they will always fail in the future:

1. Gold is a commodity. It is an investment that increases in value. To sell it based on that premise requires a securities license. Without one you are in violation of laws set forth by the SEC. G&S programs simply have no way of preventing their distributors from "speculating." Even if the company itself makes no promise of a future gain in value of the gold or silver, their ten thousand unlicensed, independent agents out there inevitably will.

As it is, I've rarely seen this angle avoided by even the companies. Yes, they themselves usually hype the investment value of their "product." They may not come right out and say it will be worth more in the future, but many of them do say it was worth less in the past. The SEC doesn't play semantic games like that.

This investment angle also places the entire MLM industry in jeopardy as well. There is already a fear that the SEC would like to regulate all MLM opportunities as investments. There is an ongoing push throughout the industry to separate the terms "investment" and "network marketing" as far apart as possible. G&S programs slam them both together.

2. Most G&S programs (but not all) usually have a system that involves the exchange of cash and commissions being paid well before a tangible product is actually received. Whether it be a voucher system, a lay-away system, a down payment, or whatever, many of them allow you to submit funds and in some manner build toward the actual purchase of gold or silver coins. In the meantime though, commissions are being paid out of those funds received and a product isn't being delivered.

3. The price of gold is the price of gold. The most anyone can get it for is whatever the going rate is. This doesn't leave

much room for mark-up. So how do you suppose G&S programs pay out 50% or more in commissions? Evidently, many federal and state regulators are assuming it's coming out of the next participant's initial down payment.

So number one involves securities violations, number two violates pyramid statutes, and number three would likely be classified as a Ponzi scheme.

Is it any wonder G&S programs rarely last more than two years?

Discount Buyers Services

Consumer's Buyline—Gone. Mainstreet Alliance—Gone. Life Plan Corporation—Gone. Personal Wealth Systems—Gone (absorbed actually). Success America—Gone. United Buyer's Service—Gone. Shopper's Advantage—Gone. American Benefits Plus—Gone. FundAmerica—Gone. Team USA—Gone. Passport to Adventure—Gone.

Over and over and over.

To my knowledge, there are only three such programs still in existence (as of this writing). One has added many other products and services to its line and greatly de-emphasizes the discount buyers service now. The other two, despite pretty much having the entire country to themselves, are struggling badly.

These services typically cost about twenty bucks to administer and routinely cost between $250 and $550 per year when purchased through the above MLM companies. But the question is never really about value. After all, these services could easily save you far more than the annual fee paid. Where the trouble always seems to be surrounds the fact that you could pick up comparable services from numerous other sources for a fraction of the cost, or perhaps even free! So the question keeps coming up: Are you paying $399 per year for a discount buyers service, or $39 for the service and $30 per month into a pyramid scheme?

Another challenge faced by most discount buyers services is that they simply don't pay well. Most cost between $18 and $30 per month. Even assuming an 80% pay out and only a nine-level-deep matrix (most are more), you could very well be earning less than $1.80 for every person in your downline (anything less than $3.00 would be considered relatively poor).

Long-Distance Phone Services

I better start right off by saying that there are exceptions to this one. Let me qualify this. I'm only talking about LDSes that offer only long-distance service and promote themselves as stand-alone, wealth-building MLM opportunities. I'm not talking about phone debit cards, voice mail or 800-number providers, or any other such telecommunications service or product.

Some LDS programs offer a variety of other services or products. Excel Telecommunications, for example, pays commissions on generic training seminars, and a great deal of income is derived from this aspect of the program. That's why this one particular company has, in fact, endured and done well.

But whatever happened to so many of the others? Almost every one has had to battle furiously to survive. In fact, it's hard to find one that hasn't struggled.

The main reason here is that most are simply resellers. They are middlemen to the original carrier. With all the tremendous competition in the LDS industry, the multimillion-dollar advertising campaigns being waged by the "big three," and the almost absurd incentives now being offered by some companies to switch to their service, getting and keeping customers has got to be an absolute terror. Especially when those customers could bypass the reseller and get a cheaper rate directly from the original carrier.

Several months ago I was using WilTel as my long-distance carrier. I switched over to an MLM company called TeleFriend (in preparation for doing a review of the program in my newsletter) and my cost-per-minute shot up over 30%! When I called 700-555-4141 to verify my actual carrier—it was still

WilTel! TeleFriend was simply a reseller. An extra middle man. (Note: some, but very few, MLM long-distance providers are their own carrier.)

And besides, if you thought earning $1.80 per downline person was bad, get this: The average residential phone bill in the United States (according to Pacific Bell) in 1994 was $34.33. At most 10% of that is actually paid out in commission, and that must then be spread across five to seven levels of distributors. So MLM LDSes usually pay you about 50 to 75¢ for each person in your downline! It takes thousands of people to add up to anything significant.

It takes about as much time, expense, and effort to recruit someone into a LDS program as it does into a consumable product program. Why not pursue the one that takes a fourth as many recruits to achieve the same income?

Australian (Two-Up) Plans

Rather than a product or service, this is actually a type of compensation plan. A type that has literally a 100% failure rate insofar as it has never produced a "successful" MLM company. If fact, I can think of only two companies that have used this plan that have passed their second anniversary, and both are very minor players within the MLM industry.

Basically, in this type of plan, the commissions generated by the first two people you sign up are passed up to your sponsor. You don't start earning commissions until your third recruit, and even then you only earn the commissions generated by their first two recruits.

One major challenge to this plan is that it is conceptually mind-boggling.

The Aussie two-up is without a doubt the most perception-oriented plan. It looks fantastic on paper because it features huge numbers next to percent signs (of course, you're only getting paid on a fraction of your downline), and it pays these bonuses downline to literal infinity (thus creating some nifty-looking income projections on paper).

But think about this: what if you signed up two people who sponsored two, who sponsored two, and so on until your downline totaled ten thousand distributors and they all were moving a total of one million dollars per month in volume. Do you know what the combined earnings would be on all ten thousand of those distributors (including you)? That's right: A big zero!

Sure, the odds of a downline forming exactly two-by-two are totally unrealistic. But still, if there is any scenario, no matter how unlikely, where ten thousand people moving a million bucks a month in volume would not generate a single commission check—something's seriously wrong with that plan.

Australian two-ups are so unpopular that not one single company in Australia uses it!

Discussion

I hesitated to include long-distance services in this article. They "never work" as primary opportunities designed to create a substantial full-time income, but as a source of supplemental income, they're fine. And again, many such programs do routinely provide additional income by generating services beyond just long distance. So it's not so much the LDS opportunities themselves that I have a problem with, it's the way they are packaged.

Those that operate discount buyers services appear to at least have sincere intentions, at least most of them. Those that attempt them genuinely seem to think they're going to do something different to break the chain of failures. They always think they've got a better way of doing it. Maybe someday someone will find it. Thomas Edison claimed he invented the light bulb by finding and eliminating every possible way it wouldn't work. If the same holds true for MLM discount buyers services, the next one should be perfect!

Now, Gold and Silver programs are a different story. Practically every one that starts up is shut down for the exact same reasons as those in the past. These operators must know going in that they'll likely be history in a year or two. But then, it doesn't take much longer than that for a million bucks to stack up in the bank. And, of course, when the ax falls they can always blame the federal or state agency that dealt the fatal blow. "Hey, it wasn't our fault," they can exclaim. "We wanted to keep paying you your commission, but those dirty government regulators made us stop." These shysters actually end up as martyrs. And, as they feign resistance to the regulatory attacks, their victims consider them heroes!

It's almost tempting, isn't it?

My feeling about those who install Aussie two-up plans into their MLM programs is that they don't understand it. They are just as deceived by its very alluring but illusionary benefits as well. Typically, most two-up plans are changed to something else a few months after the company launches.

Some programs that use the two-up (few today) seem to acknowledge that it has some faults by overlaying other types of plans, adding various peripheral bonuses, or playing gimmicky games with it (passing up the first and third person, rotating who gets passed up, and so on). Rather than abandon an extremely flawed and discredited plan, they desperately try to fix it. Once again I have to ask—why?

For decades network marketers have been taught to duplicate what works—don't reinvent the wheel. Model yourself after your successful upline. Study what they are doing and just do the same thing. But, what happens when these distributors go out and start their own MLM companies? They try to design some kind of gimmick-laden compensation plan that no one's ever tried before and get into some kind of product niche no other MLM company is in!

Folks, there is a fifty-year-long record of what works in this business and what doesn't. There is an Everest-size mountain of precedent to look back on—to model—to duplicate. And for fifty years, standard, consumable products have worked, and almost, but not quite (there are a handful of exceptions) everything else has failed! Look at the top ten largest, most successful MLM operations. Nine sell tangible, consumable products (skin and hair care, nutritional, cosmetics, home care, and so on). Primerica Services (previously A.L. Williams) might be the only exception. At least ninety-five of the top one hundred companies also offer what their competitors derogatorily refer to as "notions, potions, and lotions." Why? Because that's what works! It's what has worked for fifty years!

I think it's funny when I hear MLM companies explain that they do not offer nutritional products because so many other companies are already offering them. That makes about as much sense as the old Yogi Berra line "Nobody ever goes to that restaurant anymore because it's always so crowded."

Look back at those companies that didn't offer tangible, consumable products. NSA is a water and air purification product company, right? Yes, that makes up about a fourth of its sales. Today, the other three-fourths is a nutritional drink. Quorum used to offer only security devices and various other electronic goods. Today Quorum has nutritional products as well. Nikken added consumables to its line of magnetic therapeutic devices, as did The People's Network to its satellite communication network. Both Personal Wealth Systems and American Benefits Plus (which offered discount and benefits packages) added personal care and nutritional products to their line in an effort to survive. The list goes on and on.

Nothing is truly new in this industry. Pretty much everything has been tried. So why don't these people just follow the same rules that we distributors have been taught to follow for half a century? Duplicate what works!

*　*　*

A few months back, a subscriber faxed an article to me by a gentleman who writes a column for a major San Diego newspaper. It's a business column that often deals with the issue of multilevel marketing. Needless to say, this guy is no big fan of our industry. Despite his position as a professional journalist, his writings on MLM are completely reactionary and based on little or no actual research into the subject. For example, his assertion that MLM can't possibly work because if we all signed up only six people each we'll recruit every human being on the face of the Earth in only a matter of weeks. Die-hard MLM skeptics, usually those who've never been involved with an opportunity and are totally ignorant of how the business really works, actually believe this is a legitimate argument when attempting to debunk the concept of MLM. Still others, even those who are fairly well versed in the MLM biz, will tell you to stay away from the older companies because they are "saturated."

This misconception of saturation, fueled by the above-mentioned article, was the motivation for the following article.

The Saturation Myth

How many times have you been told by an unscrupulous, or perhaps just naive, MLM recruiter that the "other" program you were thinking about joining was "saturated?" Perhaps you have come to such a conclusion on your own, based simply on the number of people you know in your area doing a particular program. In fact, it is quite commonly, if not universally, accepted that your chances of success in a "ground floor" opportunity are better than with an "old" company. The logic is that new companies have few distributors, whereas old ones have thousands, even millions of distributors; therefore there must be far fewer prospects.

Fortunately for companies like Shaklee, Amway, Mary Kay, and Neo-Life, this assumption is, for the most part, quite false. Let us assume that there are 200 million Americans of working age who would be considered prospects for an MLM opportunity. In other words, they are not already involved, never have been (at least seriously), and are currently employed in some type of job or business (if you don't agree with the number, use your own estimate—any really big number will work). Now, these people are your prospect base. They are your primary targets, regardless of what MLM opportunity you pursue.

Okay. So you look into Amway (the largest MLM company). Well, it has more than one-and-a-half million distributors just in the United States. More than any other MLM company.

Certainly Amway must have reached the saturation point. So you sign up with a new company with fewer than one thousand distributors nationwide. Practically the whole country is virgin territory, right? Hold on.

Has that number of prospects we just discussed, be it two hundred million or whatever you estimated, changed by even one single prospect? No. Regardless of which company you choose, there are still the exact same number of working Americans who have never, or at least not recently, been involved in MLM. The only thing you really gained, as far as your prospect base, are those million-and-a-half Amway distributors who you could now try to pirate away, if you so choose. Of course, you could still pirate them away from their upline into yours even if you joined Amway, so even that's not really an advantage (and it would be highly unethical).

Sure, some might say there are millions of ex-Amway distributors out there. What about them? Well, first, this number includes all distributors since the mid-1950s, not necessarily the ones out there now. Second, those who were in Amway years ago are not necessarily non-prospects now, and most of those who would no longer consider the opportunity most likely wouldn't consider any MLM again. Believe me, I've seen this many times. People who have completely given up on MLM usually blame it on the concept, not on the particular opportunity, and never on themselves.

The closest you will ever come to really having to deal with any kind of saturation problem is when a particular MLM is very hot in one area. But this does not defeat the myth because it would be quite naive to think that any kind of success could be achieved, in any program, without your downline ever leaving your area.

I recently read an article in which a young woman was interviewed who was vehemently criticizing her MLM company for not informing her that there were a dozen other distributors in her small town of ten thousand people. She should really have been berating her sponsor, who never told her that to be successful in this business she would have to eventually go beyond her relatively small center of influence. This, by the way, involved the same opportunity that several people in other cities were calling me about—because they couldn't find a distributor in their areas to help them!

I do realize, perception is everything. And if the perception is that a particular MLM is saturated, you will have to be prepared to deal with that objection should you decide to get involved. Short of copying this article, try something like this: Ask your prospect (and you might want to try this yourself) to make their center of influence list. This list of friends, co-workers, acquaintances, and relatives usually totals more than one hundred people, sometimes several hundred. Be sure your prospect does not include names of people already seriously committed to an MLM program because they would not be prospects for any other MLM at this time (or at least shouldn't be). Then ask your prospect to cross off all those on the list who would no longer be a prospect if they got involved with a "saturated" program. Usually, not one person gets crossed off.

Discussion

If you really think about it, saturation is rarely a bona fide objection to any particular opportunity. Would you really avoid joining a company with a million distributors because there are so few distributors left to recruit? Well, what about all those thousands of prospects who are suddenly available to you when you join that company in "pre-launch?"

Obviously, there is some other reason why you wouldn't join that old, mature company, and why you think others wouldn't as well. Imagine your dream compensation plan—the one that you would consider to be perfect for you. What are your three favorite products you would like your company to offer? If Amway, Shaklee, Neo-Life, Mary Kay, or any of the older companies out there were to suddenly adopt your plan and add your favorite products to their line, I'll bet you'd suddenly forget all about how "saturated" they are.

* * *

W ho likes to listen to sales people? When you go shopping for a car, do you enjoy having the salesperson run over to you and follow you around the lot? What about when you are contacted by a telephone solicitor? Do you usually turn off the TV, tell the kids to be quiet, and begin to listen intently?

In fact, very few of us like to be sold anything. It involves giving up something more than our money. It involves releasing some control. It's a challenge to our free will. It makes us wonder, Did I really want that item, or was I sold that item? If you know exactly what you want and you set out to obtain it, then you bought the item. No one had to sell you on the idea. It was your decision. That's different. But unless your MLM prospects come to you on their own, you will have to be one of those salespeople. You will have to find a way to sell something to them. You will have to become one of those people you usually try to avoid!

No wonder so few network marketing distributors ever actually retail anything.

Uh oh. Did I say that? How dare I brake this sacred bond of secrecy by actually admitting what every MLM company already knows. The corporate videos, the opportunity meetings, the conference calls, the training manuals—they all emphasize retailing to the hilt. The impression we get is that everybody's retailing like crazy, or at least that's what we're supposed to be doing. This perception must be maintained for obvious legal reasons, and of course if a few distributors actually do sell, so much the better. And yes, there are a few exceptions where folks actually do create a retail client base. Usually, this involves one of the several MLM companies that offer non-consumable hard goods. In some rare situations you will find distributors who retail thousands of dollars in product every month. I mean they actually sell it to someone else. What a concept!

The truth is, the vast majority of MLM distributors either personally consume their products, give them away as gifts and samples, or stack them up in their garage. What retailing is done usually involves intermittent sales to immediate family members or close friends and seldom requires even half of the distributor's minimum monthly product purchase from the company each month.

Understand, I am not saying this is right, or the way it should be, I'm simply telling you it's the way it is. In fact, I've gotten a good look at many genealogies in my life (far more than just my own), and I can tell you with absolute certainty that at least one-fourth of all the distributors in this business today didn't even order any products from their company last month, let alone resell anything.

Why? Because as a society we don't like salespeople, so we don't want to be what we don't like. Also, as a society, we can't stand rejection.

Is it any wonder that one of the most popular pitch lines for many new MLM opportunities today is "No Selling Required." Many service-based companies try to convince us that because they're not selling "lotions and potions" they aren't actually selling anything (which is a complete crock). A few product-oriented companies are starting to take the "if you can't beat 'em join 'em" approach and have designed their programs around just personal consumption (and without incident from regulatory agencies, so far).

Still, despite the trend away from selling, or at least using the word "sell," it remains the one absolute in an ever evolving fifty-year-old-industry. Whether it's long distance service, shampoo, water filters, or a business opportunity, something is getting sold. To claim otherwise is what I call . . .

The Big Lie

I hate selling. Loathe it. Like most people, I can't stand the rejection. I've been told I'm good at it, and it appears I am, but I would never want to make a career out of it. Knowing this of myself, it begs the question, "Why did you get involved with network marketing?!" Yes, seventeen years ago, something got me over this hurdle. For some reason, I got the entrepreneurial spirit and decided to get involved with a business opportunity that supposedly involved heavy retailing of products.

It appears I'm not the only one. In a study we did last year at *MarketWave,* we asked more than six hundred current and ex-distributors what they disliked the most about MLM. The most common answer? Nope, not meetings. Not ethics or company failures. It wasn't stockpiling or front-end loading. It was selling! People didn't want to have to go out and sell anything. Actually, 71% of those surveyed included something to this effect among their top three answers. Amazing, isn't it?

So what would possess what must be millions of people who hate selling, or think they can't sell, to go out and jump into a business that demands constant, effective selling skills?

The money? Sure, to some extent. But I think we should give a little credit to the American public. Most folks realize that, sure, there is the potential to make obscene wealth in MLM, but what they really expect is to earn a nice comfortable living, or just some extra spending money. And the wealth could be months or years away. Years of selling.

Actually, the answer is quite obvious. Most of these people have been convinced, at least in the beginning, that to be successful in MLM you don't have to sell anything. You get other people to sell for you!

Thinking back to my early days in MLM, that is exactly what I was told. If I build this giant organization of distributors, I'll get bonuses off of all of their sales. The problem is, all those people in your downline are being told the same thing!

Today, we see all kinds of opportunities claiming "no selling necessary." They encourage distributors to just buy and consume the products themselves, or for their families. But what exactly do you call promoting your opportunity? That area of your business probably involves the most selling skills of all.

And how about selling someone on the idea that this person can be successful in the "direct selling" industry without having to sell anything?

I hear companies claim that their video or audio will "do the selling for you." Okay. How does the video convince someone to watch the video?

Or, how about this one: "It's not selling—it's sharing." Right. "Mary, I'd just love to share some of this wonderful skin cream with you—if you'll share $24.95 with me."

My all-time favorite is: "the products sell themselves." To this day, I've never seen a bar of soap call up one of my neighbors and invite itself over for a swim. Not once. But then, it is a non-vertebrate personal care item without opposable thumbs. Maybe that's why.

Some programs claim no selling is required, and they'll even do all the recruiting for you. Of course, the only downlines they really build are theirs! There's just no free lunch.

Now, I realize that there are extremely "retail" oriented companies. Yes, they encourage hard work, and the heavy retailing of their products or services. The distributors, however, seem to have a different agenda. Many of them will go out of their way to make sure their prospect doesn't hear the company message. That would turn off that 71% who hate selling.

Actually, I shouldn't lump all those people who don't want to sell the products into this group. There are many distributors who feel that retailing is a mundane chore that will result in little more than a car payment. Recruiting, however, builds fortunes. So they blast their opportunity pitch at everyone in sight. They have no problem selling the sizzle. The retailing, again, they leave to their downline.

All of this may seem as if I'm suggesting that we should all be heavily retailing even if we could personally consume to meet our quotas. Not at all. Actually, I like the personal consumption angle. I'm simply suggesting that, regardless of how the opportunity is structured, something must get sold! If not a product, then an idea, a concept, or a dream. I don't care what your product or service is, the opportunity is a product unto itself, and you can't possibly avoid selling your product to be successful—recruiting alone won't make you a penny.

Don't be discouraged by all this if you feel you are one of those that can't sell, or dislike selling. MLM can still work for you. I'm certainly one of you, and if any of the companies I was involved with during the 1980s had stayed in business, I could have been a rich man today (although it certainly has provided a wealth of knowledge). Have your upline help you. Take some time to learn from those who are already successful. Build your confidence. Acquiring selling skills can come naturally, in time. Taking a comfortable, slower, more passive approach to your opportunity can delay your success—but better to succeed slowly than fail fast.

Discussion

On that last note, let me also emphasize that the awesome power of absolutely knowing your products and opportunity are the best (at least for you) can be an incredible, life-changing experience. When you reach this point, you will be amazed at how easy it will be to sell it to others. You may even want to!

The reaction to this article was interesting because there was very little reaction. I expected at least the retailers would object.

Writing these columns reminds me of the many years I was a baseball umpire. I always knew when I'd called a good game. As I was leaving the field no one would say a word to me. Of course, if I blew a crucial call, players and fans would always give me their overall opinion of my performance. My MLM articles work pretty much the same way. Those that believe I blew it usually don't hesitate to provide me with a short critique of my work. If no one bothers to comment I figure I called it right.

Suppose there'll be much reaction to this book?

* * *

I recently ran an ad in a major MLM trade publication. It cost me almost $800, but it pulled a total of 152 responses. Not bad, unless you don't count the forty-two that were not inquiries into my opportunity—they were solicitations to join theirs. Personally, I would never allow myself to be sponsored by someone who would mail opportunity pitches under the guise of a response to mine. Not only is this rather amateurish and unproductive, it's dumb. Think about it. If you had just invested $800 into a display ad promoting your opportunity, would you consider yourself a strong candidate to be leaving that opportunity anytime soon? Me neither.

In fact, downline pirates do a lot of things that just don't make any sense. These jokers are another major peeve of mine. Sometimes it's not so much what they're doing, but the brazen, even proud way in which they do it. I've encountered some who actually seem to enjoy wrecking the other person's organization more than they enjoy building their own. Fortunately, the extremists are rare and don't stick around long. But the amateur pirate is everywhere, and they're real easy to spot.

I finally had my fill of these losers, and the result was this article, which I very much enjoyed writing.

Downline Pirates: The Scourge of the MLM Industry

Your friends are in a multilevel marketing program. They are dissatisfied. They jumped into the first program they ever saw and had no idea what they were really getting into. They still believe in MLM, just maybe not in this particular product or program. They're looking for something else. Knowing you are also involved in MLM, they may even ask you for a recommendation. Naturally, you tell them about your program. They like what they hear—and they join.

You are *not* a downline pirate!

The picture I am about to paint of these unscrupulous individuals is not going to be a pretty one. Before brush hits canvas, I wanted to make it clear that everyone who has ever pitched his MLM program to an active distributor is not necessarily a downline pirate. Your prospect could be currently involved in a blatant money game or quasi-pyramid scheme and you only intended to show them the more honest side of the industry. Perhaps you were offering a complementary program to go along with their primary program. There are a few (only a few) valid excuses for enticing current MLMers into your program.

After the painting is done, scan it carefully. Only you can judge whether you are the viewer—or the subject.

My first experience with a downline pirate came in 1979. He was the worst kind. The kind that tries to rob you from your upline into his—in the same program! I experienced decent success in that program fairly quickly, and soon realized I was now choice meat. Not only did distributors from other companies covet my services, but this one guy even tried to get me to join his downline under a false name (my girlfriend's), and discreetly abandon my existing organization.

Despite the fact he had one of the largest organizations in the company (no doubt filled with shanghaied distributors from my organization), after the company folded, he was never heard from again. Ever.

About six years ago I came across a man in Southern California who responded to a classified ad my business partner had placed for his MLM opportunity. This prospect seemed genuinely eager to receive more information and came across as very sincere. After sending him a package of information, he called my partner only to pitch him on his own program. The brochures and video my partner sent were wasted.

Already being in an investigative mode at the time, I sent this gentleman a box filled with literature, an assortment of company brochures, many product samples, and two videos. I included a cover letter specifically requesting the return of the videos, and even included return postage. Total cost: $18.

Sure enough, he called me to tell me why his program was so much better, and tried to get me to switch. During a short discussion regarding his tactics, this jerk actually told me I was out of line for being so bent out of shape, and that I should consider my $18 loss as a "cost of doing business." He went on to admit he receives "three or four" such packages a day, and that he has his office staff "trash" them.

Unfortunately, the conversation didn't last long enough for me to find out if he had "trashed" the $3 for postage.

I recently came across a situation where a man described as a "real MLM pro" had been responding to generic ads placed by MLM lead generation services for the purpose of getting his name sent out to subscribers of the service. This "pro" doesn't even have to go out and find his victims—now they call him! I thought "pro" was short for professional!

Just today I talked with a woman who told me about her experience sending out a postcard promoting her program to an "MLM enthusiast" mailing list. She sent one thousand post-cards. She claimed she received twelve responses for more information—and forty pitches on other programs!

Again and again I see information sheets that are designed specifically to recruit people from one program into another. There is always the side-by-side comparison of the comp plan, and occasionally even a comparison of products.

So who are downline pirates? Why do they do what they do? What are the repercussions?

First and foremost, a downline pirate is L-A-Z-Y!

I wrote an article (that appears elsewhere in this book) titled "The ABC Technique," which describes the three parts of the recruiting process. A, you must open the prospects' minds to getting involved in their own business. B, once opened, you must remove any preconceived ideas the prospect may have regarding MLM specifically. By step C, the prospect should be much more receptive to hearing about your actual opportunity. To some extent or another, you must always work through these three stages. And the first two may require the most work of all. Of course, if you prospect only those in someone else's downline, then someone else has already done the hardest work for you!

A downline pirate is a *coward*!

One of the hardest parts about this business is either finding people who are interested in MLM, or interesting them in it. This process may involve a lot of rejection, and perhaps even ridicule. Let's face it, it's real easy to find people who are open-minded about MLM—in someone else's downline.

A downline pirate is *naive*!

Anyone who thinks he or she can build a successful organization by loading it with people who are willing to move over as a result of a better pitch is in for a first-class education on attrition. Why do such people think they are the only downline pirates out there? Don't they realize their people are going to eventually get pitched by someone else? What do you think they're going to do the first time another "better" opportunity comes along? That's right. Poof!

The serious, committed people are—committed.

A downline pirate is a *hypocrite*!

The same clown who spent days hyping all the reasons why you should change programs will inevitably preach to you about loyalty, commitment and long-term vision—the moment someone tries to pirate you away from them.

A downline pirate is a *success pirate*!

Not only does stealing someone's downline reduce that person's chances for success, but you may be setting back the pirated distributor as well. Every downline organization, if worked consistently, will eventually take on a momentum phase much like an MLM company. Remember, if you recruited just one person a month, and 40% a month did nothing and dropped out, and the other 60% did no better than you, you would have only about forty people in your downline after one year—and more than ten thousand halfway through your fourth year.

Every time you switch to another program, you start over on the time-line. As long as you keep switching, you'll never get to the point where geometric progression kicks in, no matter how many you recruit personally. Downline pirates are doing you no favors!

They aren't doing the industry any favors either. MLM needs new blood. We must increase our numbers by attracting more professional people from outside our little world. The timing has never been better for America to discover, en masse, the value of what MLM has to offer this country. One reason why it just hasn't happened (yet) might be the way this industry feeds on itself. We, in general, seem content to just keep recycling the same people over and over and over, until they drop out.

For the most part, those entering MLM for the first time just enter the same cycle along with everybody else. And the number of new people coming in isn't exceeding those going out by much. Sure, we've seen the number of MLM participants increase by five times what it was ten years ago. But this isn't really impressive at all considering the state of our economy and what MLM has to offer it, the immense size of the untapped market of prospects, and good ol' geometric progression. Consider this: Over the same ten-year period, the number of people operating home-based business has increased by more than twenty times!

From my own experience I can tell you that the reason why all these tens of millions of new home-based entrepreneurs haven't chosen MLM as their vehicle is not just skepticism—many of them just don't know about it!

In my daily life I come across many people who are not only not involved in MLM, they are completely oblivious to it. I don't mean they don't understand it, or know of only Amway and Mary Kay, I mean they literally never heard of it! How can this be? There are six million people out there promoting their opportunities with the most powerful form of advertising available—the spoken word! And they've been doing it for decades. Maybe it's because so many network marketers are only speaking to each other!

A downline pirate is *unethical*!

Some may argue that MLM distributors are free agents. They are free to take, and be offered, a better deal. It could be said that corporate headhunters "pirate" employees from other companies all the time. Why should MLM be any different? Considering distributors are independent contractors, it should be even more acceptable, shouldn't it?

Let's not forget the differences between MLM and the corporate structure. If you quit your job to take a position with another company, the company simply replaces you. Your departure would most likely have little or no effect on your boss's income, or his boss above him, or her boss above her. In MLM, when you pirate a distributor away from another downline, you're essentially stealing money from their upline. You may very well be directly impacting their sponsor's ability to earn a livelihood, and their sponsor's sponsor as well.

Okay, sure. It may be legal. But that doesn't necessarily make it right.

A downline pirate is a *lousy mentor*!

This is a business of duplication. You do what successful distributors before you have done. Downline pirates who raid other people's organizations may appear to be successful recruiters to their downlines. Their downlines may even assume the role of downline pirate by example, even without the encouragement of their pirate sponsor. Pirating breeds more pirating.

A downline pirate is *doomed to fail*!

I've never seen a single example of a downline built through picking the fruit of other people's labor that has endured. Their "tree" may grow for a short time, but inevitably the harvester of this fallen or unripened fruit is provided sustenance for only a short time. After the fruit has gone sour or has been devoured, nothing is left. And the pirate is off to harvest more.

Successful organizations have roots. They are primarily based on seeding, nurturing, and growth.

A PICKED LONG-STEM ROSE WILL ONLY LAST SO LONG—A ROSE BUSH WILL CREATE BEAUTY FOREVER IF PROPERLY CARED FOR.

Again, I must reiterate: Just because you've sent postcards to an "MLM enthusiasts" mailing list, or advertised in an MLM trade publication that is read primarily by people already in MLM, doesn't necessarily mean you are a downline pirate. Many of these people are still in the searching stage, and there will always be a high percentage of those that are already in

MLM who are in transition—by their own accord. We're talking about the career pirate here. The jerks who feed exclusively, or at least primarily, on other people's organizations. The guy who is always looking to go one-on-one with anybody he can, to try to talk them out of their program (any way he can) and into his.

So the picture has been painted. Look at it carefully. Do you see a depiction of what is wrong with this industry? Is it an illustration of what to avoid? An image of what to not be a victim of? For some of you it may still appear to be nothing more than a white canvas, garnering no reaction at all. Still, to others, it's a self-portrait.

Discussion

Despite the many times I tried to explain what a downline pirate was not, I still got challenges from readers who felt I had unjustly described them. The "unethical" section was the main target. These folks felt I was accusing them simply because they routinely offer their opportunity to prospects who are already involved in MLM. Not true.

Perhaps there is one other differentiation that I did not expound on quite enough. As I said, many MLMers are probably dissatisfied with their current program and wouldn't mind hearing about an alternative. Even if they're doing well and shouldn't be looking elsewhere, if they make it clear they are, then they're fair game. But pirates will hit on anybody. They'll always go for the weak and vulnerable (those who are struggling and unsure about their program), but their prey of choice are the enthusiastic go-getters. The up-and-comers. Pirates have even been known to try to latch their claws into a heavy hitter or two.

Of course, to successfully snag those who are not looking for alternatives (like people who place $800 ads, send out $18 sample kits, or mail out one thousand hand-labeled letters), pirates must first destroy their targets' trust and enthusiasm in their current MLM program. That's the key distinction! Pirates feel the need to create doubt, to cause you to seek out alternatives. They tear down before they build up. That makes them easy to spot. You will know you're talking to pirates if they devote a lot of time to why you should leave your current program rather than to why you should join theirs.

My philosophy is this:

IF YOU CAN'T SUCCESSFULLY RECRUIT BY STICKING ONLY TO THE GOOD THINGS ABOUT YOUR OPPORTUNITY, THEN YOU NEED TO FIND AN OPPORTUNITY WITH MORE GOOD THINGS ABOUT IT.

4

The Numbers Game

It has been said ad nauseam that MLM is a numbers game. Probably because it is. Everything about this business is based on numbers. There are the number of prospects, number of recruits, total number of distributors in your downline, number of distributors necessary to achieve a certain stage or rank in the compensation plan, number of levels, group volume totals, personal volume requirements, commission percentages, attrition rates, company sales volume, number of years in business, number of products in the line, price of the products . . . numbers, numbers, numbers!

In one of my favorite quotes by Mark Twain, he says, "There are three kinds of lies. Lies, damn lies, and statistics!" One of my former business partners put it even better: "If you torture the data long enough you can make it say anything."

Network marketing is an absolute chamber of horrors when it comes to the practice of number crunching. On a quiet night, if you listen real hard, you can almost hear all the pocket calculators across the country screaming out in agony. Try it on a Thursday night around 8:00 P.M. That's when most of the MLM opportunity meetings are wrapping up.

One of my many majors in college was statistics. I was the statistician on my bowling team (I averaged 6.74 strikes per game!). When I was a kid I actually used to do a statistical analysis comparing the performance of Hot Wheels, Johnny Lightning, and Matchbox cars. Hot Wheels always won until it went to cheaper wheels. Today it's about even with Matchbox. Well, I'm guessing of course.

The Baseball Encyclopedia? I read it, cover to cover—last Tuesday night.

In 1990 and 1991 a few MLM companies were pretty much giving their distributors free rein to produce their own marketing and promotional material—and these distributors were going absolutely nuts with it. Some of the stuff that was coming across my desk back then would have made Einstein's hair stand on end (maybe he'd seen it already).

The result was a series of three articles I wrote in an attempt to enter the dungeons of MLM and free the data from its misery. My first effort was titled simply . . .

Multilevel Marketing: The Myth Behind the Numbers

I have always been a strong advocate of multilevel marketing. I firmly believe that if it's done ethically and intelligently it can be, for most people, the only way they can ever become financially independent. How many other vehicles to wealth can you think of that involve less than $500 of start-up capital, can be pursued part-time, involve no major financial or emotional risks, and require little or no experience or special skill? The Lottery and the Publishers Clearing House Sweepstakes maybe. That's it.

I preface this column with a positive note because I am not implying that this form of business is not viable and legitimate. When it comes to the numbers that are presented in many opportunity meetings and some promotional videos I have seen, however, some blatantly false assumptions are made! Or, at the very least, they lead unknowing prospects into accepting certain theories that do not apply in real life.

For example, any of you involved with MLM have undoubtedly seen the "If five get five, and they get five" demonstration. It proposes that all you have to do to be successful in MLM is recruit five people who get five, who also get five, and so on. By the sixth level, they say, you'll have 19,530 people in your group (this is all based on an actual example I recently saw in a recruiting video for a major MLM company). But, of course, there is a high attrition rate in MLM (they'll humbly admit, thus giving the presentation more credibility) so we'll assume 90% of your people drop out. That will leave you with 1,953 who, let's say, all do only $100 per month (absurdly optimistic). Even if you are paid a relatively low 10% commission on your entire group's volume (which is actually quite high) you will still be making $19,530 dollars a month!

Okay, so what's wrong with this picture? Well, besides the unrealistic sales and commission figures, it assumes that all 19,530 people get in before even one gets out, then all 90% drop out at once! If you are going to assume a 90% drop out rate, you must assume it from the beginning. In other words, four, or perhaps all five of your original first level people are going to drop out! In reality, the average "active" percentage in most MLMs is about 25%, with 25% pursuing it on a limited basis while the other 50% dabbles and drops out quickly. Please don't misunderstand. I do not question the monthly income figure, for it is quite realistic for someone working the business full time who's been doing it a while. What few people will tell you is that you may have to sponsor twenty-five people to find five that will go out and sponsor five others. And they'll have to do the same.

Another problem with this, or any downline projection, is that it assumes your group's hierarchy is pyramid shaped. Not only are legitimate MLM companies not pyramid schemes, their structures are not even pyramids. They're diamonds! Think about this. If your downline organization were to form a perfect pyramid you'd eventually have thousands of distributors on your bottom level and not one would have recruited a single person below them. So the "pyramid myth" is that one night you'll have one thousand people on level five and no one on level six, and the next morning you'll suddenly have five thousand on level six. Boom, just like that.

The reality is that, regardless of the size of the downline, the shaded areas shown in Figure 4.1 represent distributors who

Figure 4.1 *The mythical pyramid downlines are actually diamond-shaped.*

never really exist. The effect on your monthly income, using the previous example, is that you will actually only earn $9,765 per month with a six level downline (if only all of us could suffer such disappointment, huh?). To achieve an actual income of $19,530 would require not 1,953 distributors (which would only account for the top half of the diamond), but possibly as much as twice that number.

This isn't all the funny stuff that goes on. Some MLM companies take advantage of this false logic and load up the highest commission rates on the bottom levels. You're supposed to think you're getting the greatest bonuses on the most number of people. Actually, the greatest number of distributors, for most people, will be somewhere in the middle levels of your organization.

Also, watch out for programs that pay out on more than seven levels (unless it's a narrow matrix, then no more than twelve). The more levels, the less commission is paid on each level, including the ones where you will most realistically have most of your people. The company can only pay out so much in commission. A few months ago I got a crude, photocopied brochure in the mail regarding a "fantastic" new ground-floor MLM opportunity selling magazines through the mail. They offered an "absolutely unheard of" 10% commission down twelve levels. You can't pay 120% commission! At least you can't and stay in business. If this was a legitimate business (which it wasn't), they were obviously anticipating very little participation on the bottom levels.

I also get a kick out of those companies who claim to offer an "infinity bonus." This is a bonus of usually 1% to 15% on your entire group's volume, all the way down to infinity—or the next person downline who also qualifies for the "infinity" bonus, whichever comes first. One infinity bonus earner will block all or part of the upline's infinity bonus. In other words, an infinity bonus is a bonus that pays down to a certain point and then stops.

I looked up *infinity* in the dictionary. Mr. Webster and I seem to have a very different definition of the word than most MLM companies do.

One of my biggest peeves is companies that claim low attrition rates among their distributor base, along the lines of 5% to 15%. Notice that these companies never tell you what time period they're basing these figures on. Is it 5% a month? A year? Over the life of the company? It makes a *big* difference. I've even seen an ad for a new MLM company that was claiming "Zero attrition." I also knew the ad deadline for that publication. It was three weeks after the company's official launch date. Of course they had zero attrition—everyone just signed up!

There are very good, honest companies out there whose distributors still use this five-by-five scenario for demonstration purposes, claim they pay down infinite levels, or boast low attrition rates. Many of them are genuinely unaware of the inaccuracy of their information. I'm not suggesting you avoid those companies or distributors who use these tactics. I'm simply hoping that with this information you will be more aware of the false logic employed here, not only to present your opportunity with less risk to you and your company's credibility, but to pursue your MLM career with more realistic expectations as well.

* * *

This next article pretty much applies to the majority of MLM companies out there, and I expect they are not going to like it. If this book gets labeled "controversial," you could probably point your finger right here. But we've come this far, no sense backpedaling now.

Kissing Up to the Heavy Hitters

If all of us were in a room together, and I asked you to raise your hand if you had ever involved in an MLM opportunity, just about all hands would go up. If I then asked only those who had made any money at it, even a few hundred dollars a month, to keep their hands up, the wind created by all those arms dropping at the same time would probably blow me over!

Why is that?

You get customers with a product. You get distributors with a compensation plan. And what do most companies, and just about all distributors, do to convince you how lucrative their comp plan is? They tell you three things: how many levels it pays, what the total pay-out percentage is, and what the highest earners are making.

Comp plan design is without a doubt the most perception-oriented aspect of any MLM business opportunity. There are tons of ways of making a plan appear more lucrative on paper, which in reality pays no more than any other plan.

Most plans are designed to pay out potentially more than 50% (in some cases even 80%, 90%, or even more than 100%) in commissions, and some plans even pay down as many as forty-nine levels! The claim of "infinite depth" is now popular in all types of plans. Of course, most claim to pay down infinitely to only a certain point and then stop. How many times have you heard, "You are paid down an infinite number of levels to your next qualified (manager, executive, whatever)."

Probably the best way to demonstrate the income potential of your plan is to show off those few who are earning high five-, or even six-digit monthly incomes.

Let's say the top earner for Company A is making one million dollars per month (it's happened, folks), and the top earner for Company B is earning $50,000 per year. Which compensation plan would you assume is the most lucrative? What if I told you that Company A had ten thousand distributors, and only one was making one million per month? The other 9,999 were all broke. Company B on the other hand, had one hundred distributors making $50,000 per year, and another five hundred making $1,000 per month, and the rest were all making a few hundred dollars. An exaggerated example, obviously. But the point is this: Armed only with the knowledge of what the top earner was making, about 99% of all new distributors would join Company A—and about 99% of them would make far less money!

THERE'S A *BIG* DIFFERENCE BETWEEN REALISTIC, ACHIEVABLE INCOME, AND POTENTIAL, THEORETICAL INCOME.

So designing a plan that pays "infinitely," or that pays eight or nine (or forty-nine) levels instead of the standard five or six, and that has a potential pay out of 55%, or 76%, or 138%, kills two birds with one stone. Not only does it make for a great income projection on paper (which is the worst place to compare comp plans—they all make you rich on paper), but a very few "heavy hitters" will actually achieve the "back-end" of the plan, and make gazillions of dollars.

Some companies are so desperate for a heavy hitter to showcase around the country that they will simply create one! Some manage this by placing the heavy hitters on the corporate front line, then building or transferring large numbers of distributors under them. This is one reason why heavy hitters with one company switch over to another. It's rarely because they willingly chose to abandon $30,000 in monthly residual income just to start over from scratch with a "better" opportunity, as they'll tell you. That's ridiculous.

Some companies feel they are at such a marketing disadvantage by not having a heavy hitter, they will fake one! This is rare, but it does happen.

I've designed comp plans for several start-up opportunities. At one time, early on, I proposed a type of comp plan that would dramatically increase the number of people making a few hundred dollars per month, quadruple the number of folks earning comfortable full-time incomes, but have little or no potential to ever create a millionaire. In almost every case the idea was resoundingly rejected. The common reason for rejecting the plan was always the same—it wouldn't attract the "heavy hitters."

As the supply of opportunities continues to outstrip the demand, the competition for distributors is becoming fierce. Companies are trying every way they can think of to create the perception that their plan pays more, and in more ways than what I have mentioned here—for example, by adding more awards and incentives, such as bonus pools for the top recruiters, personal volumes, and group volumes. But in most cases, isn't this rewarding those who are already successful? Doesn't this appear to be designed, at least in most cases, to make the rich richer?

We asked the more than six thousand MLM distributors we surveyed over the last six years what the primary motivation was behind their involvement in MLM. Fifty-four percent said "to make more money," 32% answered "to have more free time," or something to that effect (more time with family, wake up later, no commuting, and so on). Of the 54% that answered "to make more money," who were asked why they wanted to make more money, 60% said "to have more free time."

We also asked specifically what income level they wished to realistically achieve in their MLM opportunity. Amazingly, more than 86% claimed they would have been satisfied with only an extra $250 per month, or to only replace their current family income ($2,500 to $6,000 per month), but have one person work twenty flexible hours a week to achieve it, rather than forty to fifty fixed hours.

They (you) keep saying the same thing! Getting up in the morning whenever you want, working from home, spending more time with your family, relaxing, spending more time on hobbies or traveling, buying a "toy" or two you've been wanting, and earning no more than a comfortable full-time income—all this is as grand a dream to most of us as is getting rich!

So why are so many comp plans designed to pay out $100,000 to $500,000 per month to a handful of heavy hitters, and leave thousands of others broke and disgusted? Think about that. If just one heavy hitter making $200,000 per month were to make $100,000 instead (assuming they could still survive on that), that would mean one hundred more distributors could earn $1,000 per month rather than break even. One thousand more distributors losing $50 per month could be making $50 (dramatically lowering attrition rates, and the number of P-O'd ex-distributors). And this is by halving just one heavy hitter check!

So what's the answer? What is a type of plan that could achieve such a sharing of the wealth, that would be so unattractive to heavy hitters? Well, here's one:

Three levels (you've got to be kidding! You can't make money in a three-level plan) that pays 2%, 2%, and 40% (only 44% total pay out?—ho hum), with a $100 personal volume (but there's no incentive to retail—forget it, people won't move any product). Allow me to answer these assumed knee-jerk responses.

Most plans that claim to pay a total pay-out of X percent actually pay about half that. For example, one well-known service program claims a total pay-out of as much as 100%, but actually pays about 55%. Another product company I worked for claims a total maximum pay-out of 49%, but actually averages between 22% and 26% pay-out each month. I'm aware of a break-away plan that claims a maximum of 58% that actually averages "well under 30%" according to their very honest and candid CEO. In the three-level plan just described, assuming only a $100 PV (monthly personal volume) qualification for full bonuses, it would pay out pretty close to the full 44% every time, thus paying out from 5% to as much as 20% more commissions, not less.

Finally, high group and personal volume requirements are *not* incentives to retail. They are incentives to purchase wholesale!

Big difference. High qualifications don't make non-salespeople (most of us) suddenly become salespeople. All they do is force people to do more of what they don't want to do—sell. Or else build an addition onto their garage to hold all their inventory.

If everyone did no more than $100, this would work. Personally consume a little, and sell a few products to Aunt Mary, your mom, and your best friend Jack, and you're probably covered. Not a real tough assignment for most of us, even those who hate to sell.

Let's put this plan to the test:

	Plan A		Plan B	
Level	Recruits	Pay-Out	Recruits	Pay-Out
1.	5	5%	5	2%
2.	25	5%	25	2%
3.	125	5%	125	40%
4.	625	5%	25	
5.	125	6%	5	
6.	25	10%		
7.	5	10%		
Total:	935	46%	185	44%

As you can see, Plan A has 750 more people (780 more you are getting paid on), pays 2% higher commissions overall, and pays four levels deeper. Plan A beats Plan B in all three areas. Plan B can't possibly pay more, right?

Wrong. Assuming a $100 PV for both, Plan A would pay $4,950, and Plan B would pay $5,060! That's with only 185 total active distributors. And this is assuming that you qualify for all seven levels of overrides in Plan A, which, in most plans, would likely require a lot more than a $100 personal volume.

Consider, in Plan A I could have reduced level five by 1%, and doubled levels one and seven to create a total pay-out of 60%, which would create the illusion that it paid even more—and your income would drop by $50 per month!

Yes, Plan A has a far greater income potential. Absolutely. All Plan B would accomplish is, at best, maybe $30,000 per month. Plan A could *potentially* pay five times this amount. Of course, the chances of earning $2,500 per month are increased (astronomically compared with most plans) in Plan B, but this is rarely a consideration when distributors compare comp plans, and many companies know it.

Why are there very few plans out there like Plan B? Because it would neither attract nor create a heavy hitter! That is in spite of the fact that the company would actually pay out more commissions overall, to more distributors. Also—it looks terrible on paper!

(Understand, I don't blame the heavy hitters themselves. Heck, I'm well on my way to being one myself. Some of my closest friends in this industry would likely be tagged with this label. I hold them about as responsible as I do those professional baseball players who accept forty-seven-million-dollar contracts. If the company is going to pay it to them, I don't expect anyone to refuse it.)

There's more to a plan like this than just more money.

Despite its advantages and relative simplicity as a business opportunity, MLM is nonetheless just that—a business opportunity. It does require some limited skills and a certain personality type to achieve real, substantial success in this business. I believe it is time for us as an industry to admit to ourselves that trying to train literally millions of non-entrepreneurs how to think and act like professional business managers, trainers, and salespeople, even to the limited extent required to be successful in MLM (compared with conventional businesses), may be an insurmountable task. Besides, the whole allure of network marketing was that you didn't have to be all of those things to be successful, remember?

Instead, perhaps we should be thinking about simplifying the business. The computer industry is a great example. Rather than trying to train millions of technophobes how to use a PC, let's design a simpler computer. It sure worked for Apple!

So employing very simple compensation plans, with easier-to-interpret, lower qualifiers (but not too low) to receive full commissions, not only puts money into the pockets of far more distributors (thus putting far more distributors into MLM), but it also creates an extremely duplicatable program that anyone, truly anyone, can at least make that extra $250 in.

Now, if companies can just get past this devotion to heavy hitters, if they would design plans for the other 99% of us, perhaps we could really start turning around this lingering image we have of being an industry full of get-rich-quick-schemes and front-loading con artists.

Break-even would occur weeks or months earlier, thus dropping attrition rates through the floor. Far more people would be running around the country talking about the money they are making in MLM, rather than how much they lost.

Personally, I also believe that reducing the number of distributors earning $100,000 per month, and increasing the number of those that earn a comfortable $50,000 per year would only add to the credibility of the industry. Not only in the eyes of the public, but also with the media and government as well. I agree this may be unjust, but that doesn't make it untrue.

Try coming up with any scenario in our $100 per month plan that would behoove someone to front-load. There's none. This practice would be completely eliminated forever!

Sure, this would also mean the extinction of the MLM millionaire. The term "heavy hitter" would still exist, but it would be redefined. But if it meant tens of thousands more of us achieving our true dream, that being personal control, time freedom, and financial security (which doesn't require great wealth) then I believe your response would be the same as mine.

So what!

Discussion

Compensation plans don't design themselves. Somebody's got to sit down and figure out who gets paid what and how much. Who do you think does that, folks? The "little guy?" Those thousands of struggling, hard-working distributors down in the trenches? Or, is it perhaps the company owners and a few of their top "heavy hitters?" Oh, an independent consultant may be hired to do the actual work. But the company calls the shots. I've seen many of them start out with a very noble, share-the-wealth philosophy, only to change the plan later once their very top distributors wanted more—or else.

I was hired to design a comp plan back in 1991 by a company that wanted to offer an opportunity for "everyone to make money." Okay. I told them I could do that, and I did. It was a nice, simple little unilevel plan. Not too many bells and whistles. About eighteen months later the company was bought out by some then-silent, limited partners. They contacted me to redesign the plan. They now wanted a very high qualification, deep level, stair-step break-away plan. The old and new plans were pretty much complete opposites in their philosophy. When I asked the new company president why he wanted to put his people through that kind of culture shock, his exact words to me were frightening. He said, "Because *we* want to make some money now."

A couple of disclaimers:

First, the fact they wanted to change to a break-away plan was not really the problem. It was the kind of break-away plan. I'm not a break-away basher by any means. There are some very "soft," very fair break-away plans out there. Some.

Second, I have no problem with MLM companies making money. In fact, I hope the company I'm with makes tons of it. I'd like them to hang around for a while. It's when they intentionally design plans to make money *instead* of the distributors that gets me. It's another one of my peeves.

I think a lot of companies could pay a lot more than they are to their distributors. But when they have a few mega-rich heavy hitters and a plan that pays a million bucks a month in theory as evidence, most distributors assume the company is paying all they can. Technically though, Monopoly money is worth more than theoretical money.

One good way of knowing when your company might have a little more room to play with in their commission expense budget is when they hire $20,000 per day guest speakers for

their national conventions—as several of the richest companies have done in recent years. Personally, I'd rather listen to a
stand-up comic do a bit about MLM for union scale ($400, last
I heard), and watch an awards ceremony where twenty hard-
working but struggling distributors received $1,000 bonuses!

I don't want to get into much detail about specific comp
plan types and their pros and cons right now. That will be the
subject of my next book. (Of course, for someone who might
soon become the Salman Rushdie of network marketing to
already be thinking sequel—well, call me an optimist.)

In general though, you should think of compensation plans
as big machines. In one end flows product volume and out the
other comes your commissions and bonuses. After all, isn't
that what a compensation "machine" is supposed to do—
convert sales volume into commissions?

It seems every MLM company is doing everything it can to
convince us that its machine is more efficient at this process
than anyone else's. To demonstrate how powerful their compensation machines are, they paint them with pretty colors
and add flashing lights, loud sirens, and all kinds of other
fancy bells and whistles. They change the shape and size of the
machines, add various accessories and attachments, and sometimes they'll even connect two or three types of machines
together (called "hybrid" plans). They'll give them bold, exciting names, make them customizable, and include an operations manual three inches thick. In fact, about the only thing
they don't provide is a lifetime warranty!

All of this effort is to create the perception that their
machines work better (pay more) than anyone else's machines.
Do they? Probably not.

Looking at this issue from the most macro view, the plain
and simple truth is that if you were to put the exact same
amount of product volume into 95% of the compensation
machines out there, just about the same amount of commissions would come out the other end. The real key is how
much volume goes in, and how and to whom the commissions
are distributed.

Look at the two commission pay-outs below. Unlike our last example, let's assume you have the exact same number of distributors on each level for both plans. Which one do you think would actually pay more?

Level	Plan 1	Plan 2
1	6%	5%
2	6%	5%
3	6%	5%
4	6%	5%
5	6%	5%
6	6%	—

At first glance, most would instinctively say Plan 1 would pay more. But what if I told you that in Plan 1 you would be selling small office supplies? Things like staples, note pads, pencils and erasers. Nothing over $2. Now in Plan 2 you would be selling high-ticket items like jewelry, water and air filters, security devices, and a line of one hundred consumable, high-quality personal care and nutritional products. Now which one do you think would actually pay more?

Okay, let's assume that in both cases you are selling the exact same products for the exact same price. Now which plan would pay more? Plan 1 you say? Well, what if Plan 1 requires $10,000 in monthly group volume, $500 in monthly personal volume, and a six-month qualification period to reach the top rank of Master Moon Rock Executive Director. To actually qualify for the 6% down all six levels, you need fifteen other first level, personally sponsored Master Moon Rock Executive Directors. To get the 5% down all five levels in Plan 2 you only have to purchase $75 worth of product each month. Sure, Plan 1 has far more income potential, but Plan 2 would clearly benefit far more people.

The qualifications to reach certain stages, ranks, or commissions levels in a comp plan are probably the most overlooked aspect of any comp plan evaluation. Don't all 5 × 5 scenarios, or just about any kind of income projection, always assume you're meeting all your qualifications? Essentially, they're saying "If" you meet all your qualifications, you'll get paid this on this size organization. That's a big "if," folks!

Most plans are worded so they don't really convey the true effort that is required to fully succeed. For example, many plans are based on "bonus volume." This is usually an amount not much less than, or equal to, the wholesale cost of the products. In some rare cases it may even be a bit higher. In a few plans, however, this amount is well under 60% of the distributor cost for many of the products. In other words, a plan that requires "$2,000 in group bonus volume" might actually require your group to spend as much as $3,000 or more in "real" money.

A better example would be a discussion I had recently with a gentleman who wanted me to critique a plan that required $9,000 in accumulated group volume (over any period of time), of which at least $2,000 occurred in one month, to reach the level of "Director." To achieve the highest pay level in the plan required him to personally recruit eight other directors into his first level. When I asked him if he understood how hard that might be (I never implied it was impossible, just hard) his response was very typical. He said, "Oh, I should be able to recruit eight people—at least!" I then asked him to estimate what percentage of all those he personally recruited would someday reach the level of director in this plan. He guessed 5%, which was reasonably optimistic (this is actually a relatively fair plan). So I said, let's be absurdly optimistic and say 10%, just to be fair. That would mean he would actually have to personally recruit eighty people, not eight, to achieve this highest stage in the comp plan. And keep in mind, I've seen plans with much tougher qualifications to reach what this plan called "director," and some demand as many as twenty of them on your first level to reach the highest paying stage.

So which sounds better: $100 per month in "bonus volume," or $200 per month in wholesale purchases? How about: Ten personally sponsored first-level directors, or one hundred personally sponsored first-level distributors? It's very possible that in each of these examples the requirements are actually equal!

I'm not suggesting these qualifications are unfair or unachievable. Most are, if you work hard and stay committed. It's the way they are presented that really bugs me. We play semantic games with our comp plans to make them appear more easily achievable, requiring only a little effort, then once our prospect has joined we sit around griping about how little effort they're putting into it. If we would all explain what's really involved with meeting certain qualifications, how much commitment and effort it really takes, maybe people would really do what it takes to meet them.

Before I leave this subject, I just thought I'd note that since this article was originally written, two companies have adopted a three-level compensation plan and I've found two others who had tried it in the past, which amazed me. This was meant as an exaggerated example of my point. I never expected anyone to actually try it. As it turns out, one of the previous companies went out of business within a year and the other abandoned the concept and went to a six-level plan. Of the two that have tried it since, one went belly up within six months and the other recently changed to a five-level plan (and is considering an "infinity" bonus).

The reason? First of all, their own distributors complained they couldn't recruit any heavy hitters. At least, that's the excuse given to me by one of these companies. I think I know the real reason, which was totally predictable. As I said earlier, the leaders in the field, the top earners with the largest downlines, tend to have a lot of influence on the design of the compensation plan. The handful of people whose downlines comprise the majority of the company's distributors are coddled and "kissed up" to, for obvious reasons.

So what do you think happens when Bob Bigshot has five thousand people in his group and he suddenly realizes that forty-five hundred of them are out of his pay range (below the third level)? Sure, Bob demands he be paid on more levels! Bob loved the strong-paying "front end" of Plan B at first, when most of his group fell within the first three levels. He was making tons more than he would have in any of those deep paying plans. But now he's making tons less, and he wants more—or he's taking his group to another company that will adequately reward him for a downline of this size.

One company operating today actually pays two levels deep, with the largest percentage on the second level, and one of those "infinity" bonuses starting at level three. Some of its "leaders" claim you can get paid $30 to $40 per distributor in your entire downline (anything over $5 is considered an extremely good paying plan). Technically, the claim is true—if you have about 120 people in your downline and one hundred of them fall on your second level. Today, after about a year in business, the "top earner" is claiming a monthly income of $21,000. Certainly nothing to sneeze at. But, he's also claiming to have more than seven thousand distributors in his downline. I think that comes out to $3 per distributor, not $30. And, naturally, as his group continues to grow, mostly downward beyond the pay range of the plan, his earnings per distributor ratio will continue to drop. Certainly this phenomenon could also occur in a six- or seven-level plan, but months or years later.

This would be considered an extremely "front-end" heavy plan. If all you want to do is make a few hundred dollars per month, this type of plan is perfect. Most MLM distributors, however, have a goal of earning a "comfortable, full-time income" which, when quantified and averaged, comes out to $5,988 per month (based on our surveys). A "middle-weighted" plan would be far more conducive to this financial agenda. In fact, a two- or three-level plan would likely make it considerably harder to achieve this income.

So, again, Plan A (page 134) was an intentionally exaggerated example to demonstrate a point. It should be obvious to anyone who has done the homework that such plans don't work in the real world, in the long run. Yet, in an effort to impress the Little Guy, some extremist companies have gone way too far. Although their intentions are noble, their methods are naive.

By the way, the MLM program I just described added a new bonus recently to its plan—it pays on deeper levels.

Please understand that a number of good MLM programs exist today that have found an appropriate middle ground. And, they come with all different types of plans (unilevel, break-away, matrix, and binary). Also, I am not suggesting that front- or back-end heavy plans are better or worse, good or bad, or right or wrong. That's for you to decide based on what you want. You must decide which compensation plan "philosophy" best suits you and your goals. Unfortunately, most distributors will tell you that their plans are all things to all people. You need to know the true nature of the plan.

Here are some guidelines to help you better judge the true income potential of an MLM program:

What is the volume potential? Few distributors new to the MLM industry seem to understand that when their company's computer calculates their commission check that there is a number on both sides of the multiplication sign. It's sales volume times commission percentage equals your income. So the equation is SV × CP = I. Or, a better way to look at it is like this: P × C = I. In other words, *Products × Comp Plan = Income*. Most distributors today only seem to concentrate on the "C" side of the equation. How big are the percentages? What do they all add up to? How many levels deep do they go? What type of plan is it?

Ninety percent of any discussion revolving around income is focused on the compensation plan. Of course, a plan could pay 10% down fifty levels, with a total pay-out of a whopping 500%—and 500% of zero would be zero! I believe it's the product volume side of the equation that is as, if not more, important than the compensation plan in determining the true income-generating ability of the program. If enough volume flows through it, any plan will pay well. No volume and the best-looking plan in existence will fail within weeks.

How achievable are the qualifications?   It really makes no difference how high the pay-out of a plan is if you can't meet the quotas to qualify for it. The qualifications tend to get over-looked by the prospect, or underemphasized by the prospector. Remember, base your judgment on how achievable a plan is on the assumption that you intend to work it for at least a year or two. And don't forget—there is such a thing as too easy. A plan should require at least some amount of effort and long-term commitment.

Where are the commissions weighted?   Rather than focusing on how high the percentages are or what they all add up to, pay more attention to where they are. As you contrast and compare more and more compensation plans, you will be able to better determine what are front, middle, or back-end weighted plans.

Place little or no value on earnings claims!   First, don't trust 'em. Some MLMers have a habit of manipulating this data to their advantage (that is, counting gross income before they've paid their downline, not revealing that they earned their hefty income so quickly by moving a large chunk of their existing downline over from another company, and so on).

Second, income level is more a matter of how long someone has been in an MLM program, not how well that program pays. When I first joined my MLM program, I hated being asked how much I was making. Of course I was making very little. I just joined, for crying out loud! Today I'm doing very well, but I've been doing it for almost two years full time (with this particular company). In fact, one of the richest network marketers I know is working what would be, in my opinion, one of the weakest paying programs—but he's been working it for more than twenty years! On the other hand, MLM superstars such as Mark Yarnell, Venus Andrecht, and Ken Pontius likely made very little income—their first month in the business.

* * *

This next article is one of my all-time favorites. It was a joy to research and to write. It actually was something I'd been working on for several months. As I waded through mountains of MLM material each week, I took notes of any "data tortur-ing" I came across and put it into my "torture file." Keep in mind, most of this was just from material I'd found during the last half of 1993. And the best thing about this article is that I finally got to use the title . . .

If You Torture the Data Long Enough, You Can Make It Say Anything

About twenty years ago, as part of an assignment for a high school civics class, I was required to attend a jury trial. I have little memory of that hearing other than it involved a medical malpractice suit—and one of the all-time classic examples of data torturing.

During that trial, I recall there being an accusation that a monitor that measured some particular vital sign was ignored even when it began to fluctuate. The prosecution displayed a chart of the line as it appeared on the monitor, with the verti-cal axis to the left, and measured in increments of 0.1, 0.2, 0.3, all the way to 1.0. The line looked like a silhouette of the Himalayas. The defense attorney also brought along a chart displaying the same line, but using the same scaling of the ver-tical axis that appeared on the monitor itself, which was 0.5, 1.0, 1.5, 2.0, and so on. The line now displayed a couple of lit-tle ant hills.

Understand, both attorneys presented completely factual information, based on the exact same data.

Of course, the defense attorney's earlier objection to the "adjusted" chart was sustained. The jury was instructed to dis-regard the chart, but no clear explanation was given to them, and they did seem confused. This amazed me, for the fallacy here seemed so obvious. Of course, these were twelve people who also couldn't figure out how to get out of jury duty. Let's give 'em a break.

Here's an example of how this same ploy is sometimes used by MLM companies. Figure 4.2 represents the annual sales of the make believe XYZ company over the six years it's been in business. Take note of the scaling of the vertical axis.

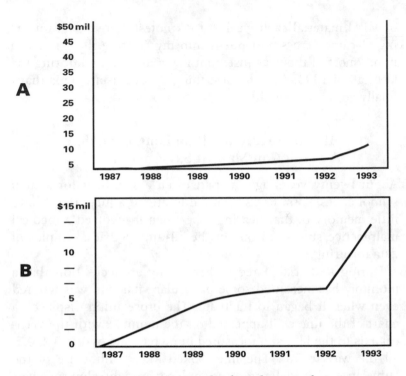

Figure 4.2 This is a prime example of graph manipulation.

In graph A, note the slight increase in sales during the last year.

Now, let's take a look at graph B, which represents the exact same sales figures but with an altered scaling of the vertical axis. What happens?

They're suddenly in *Momentum!* They're *Exploding!* They're *Hot!* Better get in now. This company is *Going Through The Roof!*

Another great example of graph torturing can be found among the literature I've been receiving for an MLM vitamin company. Figure 4.3 is an approximation of a graph it's presented that shows the nutrient level within the bloodstream when vitamin tablets are used, compared with its vitamin spray. (Because this is a rather litigious company, I'm not using the actual graph, but rather a close approximation.)

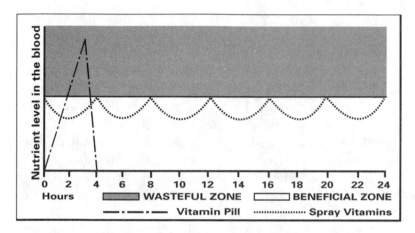

Figure 4.3 Another example of graph manipulation.

Notice, it's comparing one dosage of vitamin tablets to several doses throughout the day of it's spray. This is like comparing the hunger levels of someone who ate once in the morning to someone who had three full meals. And notice the curious upswings in nutrient levels that occur about an hour before each dosage of the spray. Exactly how does that happen?

Another example was a graph that was recently published in a popular national magazine that accompanied an article by a top distributor for a well-known MLM company. He was comparing the virtues of the break-away plan with the matrix plan. In an effort to demonstrate the advantages of the break-away plan, he displayed a graph showing the number of people that would fall on each level in a 3 × 4 matrix compared with that of an unlimited width break-away plan. Not only did he choose an extremely weak form of matrix that doesn't exist anywhere in the industry, but he also compared the numbers it would generate to his actual downline! Keep in mind, a 3 × 4 matrix would only accommodate 120 people, and the author's actual organization exceeds thirty-five thousand. Making this comparison is like saying Chevrolets are faster than Fords by comparing a Corvette with a Pinto. Or, that the American League is better than the National League by comparing the 1927 Yankees to the 1962 Mets.

Graph fudging isn't always used to promote; it's sometimes used to detract. For example, when *Forbes* magazine attacked Herbalife some months back, the magazine displayed graphs showing how sales figures in four foreign countries had risen, then fallen. Of course, U.S. sales had risen, then fallen—then risen again! Also, Herbalife is in fifteen countries, and it seems as if only those where this severe drop occurred were chosen to be represented in this graph. What about the other eleven countries?

This practice of companies only picking targets that serve them is also widespread. I recall some years ago, a now defunct MLM company was comparing the price of their laundry detergent with that of three other name brands. It beat the price of all three, giving the impression it offered the best price. What I discovered was that there were thirteen brands available at my local supermarket, and those three name brands were, in fact, higher in price—and the other ten were lower! The MLM product was actually the fourth most expensive.

Then there's the mysterious crystal ball graph. These have "projected" sales for the following year with a line that goes practically straight up at the end. It seems practically every MLM company is going to go into a massive momentum phase next year.

I also can't stand to read about a three-month-old company claiming to have monthly sales increases of 3000%. Think about that. It could have sold $10 the first month, another $10 the second, and $4,000 the third, which would be a "3000% increase," but still be pitiful overall sales. The percentage of increase means very little. It's how much it sold that counts.

Many companies claim that so many thousands of new distributors are signing up each month. Notice, they never tell you how many are dropping out. A thousand new recruits a month is great—unless fifteen hundred are leaving.

I've been hearing a lot lately about companies that claim to have signed up, say, one thousand people their first month, and now have two thousand after four months. The implication is that they're still growing, which is technically true. But look at it this way: They signed up one thousand their first month, and an average of 333 in each of their next three. Recruitment is actually dropping.

Claims of low attrition rates are another great peeve of mine. Notice that companies that claim a drop-out rate of less than 10% never tell us what time period that's based on. Is that 10% a year? A month? A day? Some companies simply never purge their database, or they offer a one-time enrollment fee for a "lifetime distributorship." This is simply a matter of changing the rules to make the statistic fit. It's like making everything legal and claiming a zero percent crime rate!

And what about this newest myth going around that the Direct Selling Association (DSA) claims that the average MLM distributor recruits 2.7 people? For years the figure was 2.6, allegedly taken from some research a top NuSkin distributor had conducted several years ago. Our survey of more than six thousand MLMers over the last six years came up with 2.1.

Guess what? We're all wrong. It's mathematically impossible for this number to be greater than one. Really think about this stuff. If every distributor that ever joined an MLM opportunity over the last 50 years recruited an average of even two others, we would, in fact, have recruited every man, woman, child, statue, mannequin, snowman, and crash dummy on the face of the earth. A few years ago parents were literally fighting over Cabbage Patch Kids. If the previous scenario were true—we'd now be fighting over who recruits them!

Ninety-five percent failure rate among MLM companies within the first two years? Wrong! Show me any research, any evidence at all that will back up that figure. It's simply propaganda perpetuated by distributors of older, mature companies, or those promoting an MLM portfolio. Our records over the last six years indicate a failure rate of about 80%, which is consistent with conventional businesses, and about 80% of those who fail do so within the first year. But let's assume for the moment that the "95% fail in the first two years" claim is accurate. Couldn't we also claim that "95% of all MLM companies fail in the first 20 years" and be stating an absolute truth? (Of course, you'd only say that if you were in a twenty-one-year-old company.)

Data torturing can be found in product claims as well. For example, how many times have you heard the claim "Contains 100% pure Aloe Vera!" A recent study concluded that the majority of aloe products (from any source, not just MLM) actually contain only a small amount of actual aloe. Very few with this claim were genuinely pure aloe products. But does that mean they were lying? Not at all. If I take a teaspoon of "100% pure aloe vera" and pour it into a ten-gallon vat of water, does that vat not "contain 100% pure aloe vera?" It sure does—along with ten gallons of water.

Probably my biggest gripe is with those companies that try to create the illusion that their plans pay more by devising a pay-out where the total of all the percentages on each level add up to some incredible number, like 75% or 88%. What if I designed a plan that paid 1% down 90 levels? Wouldn't this plan have a total maximum pay-out of 90%? Yes, and it would also be one of the most pathetically paying plans in history. A ridiculous example, obviously. But to a lesser degree, such tactics are being employed every day in this business (by some companies, not the majority).

Semantics play a big role in data torturing as well. For example, Mary Kay Cosmetics reps claim MK has created more women millionaires than any other company in America. The top earner in Mary Kay earns about $500,000 per year, however. MK is referring to lifetime earnings. If that's the case, then just about all of us are going to be millionaires someday.

I know a guy who has publicly stated he's had "over 70,000 people in my organization." Actually, he's never had more than 6,000 at one time. He's referring to all the distributors he's ever had, which sounds a lot better, doesn't it?

Or, how about this claim: "Acme International is approaching $10 million in monthly sales!" If Acme did $1,000 in sales in January and $1,500 in sales in February, are they not "approaching" $10 million in monthly sales?

A couple years ago, a company claimed that 93% of all those surveyed had lost weight on their diet products. What wasn't revealed was that only those who had been on the product for at least six months were part of the survey. What I can't figure out is why the other 7% kept ordering!

I'm certainly not suggesting that every statistical claim made in this industry is bogus or misleading. In fact, most are not. But we as a group, meaning us MLMers, really need to stop taking everything on faith. Think about what you are told. Question it. Even suspect it.

When you and your family's personal and financial well-being are at stake, there's nothing wrong with assuming a little guilt until innocence is proven.

Discussion

One currently hot MLM company (as of this writing) is claiming it has amassed three hundred thousand distributors in the first four years. Another is claiming eighty-seven thousand in the first eighteen months. What they're not telling anyone (unless you ask, as I did) is that they have yet to purge their database of inactive or retired distributors. They don't currently have three hundred thousand or eighty-seven thousand distributors. What they have are that many total distributor applications—including those of people who have quit months or years ago. One has no enrollment fee to be a distributor and absolutely absurd retail pricing. So thousands of those being counted as "distributors" are really just wholesale customers who sign up just to get the product cheaper. This same company is also claiming monthly sales of $8.5 million, but that's based on its ridiculous 100% suggested retail mark-up. Therefore, sales are actually $4.25 million.

Several companies use what is called a "binary" compensation plan. In general, I don't really care for binaries, although this type of plan does offer some unique advantages. But one alleged advantage it really does not have is that it pays "infinitely" in depth. After some mathematical analysis, I discovered that the commission portion of any particular sale was approximately halved each level upline. In other words, if the company wanted to pay $50 in commissions to the field on a $100 purchase, $25 would be paid to the first level upline from the sale, then $12.50 to the next qualified person above them, then $6.25, then $3.13, and so on up the line—theoretically forever! Why? Because any number in the universe, no matter how small it gets, can still be divided by two, correct? So does it really pay infinitely? Yes, if you don't mind earning .00005¢ on a $100 sale on your 20th level.

I guess the previous article was an example of torturing the data until it tells the truth!

* * *

Being a distributor myself, I'm often asked various statistical questions about my opportunity. Although most are fair and valid questions, I used to hate having to answer them (though I always did). The reason is that in this business, at least until recently, you tended to place yourself at a marketing disadvantage by telling the truth. I'm always concerned that my truths may not be as good as the other guy's hype and exaggerations.

Personally, over the last couple of years or so, I've found that a shift is occurring in the diligence levels and expectations of most new MLM prospects. Hype is out, truth is in. Those "outer circle" folks looking at MLM for the first time seem to have become a pretty jaded, more professional group overall. More and more of them are following the "opportunity seekers" Golden Rule: If it sounds too good to be true, it probably is. To these folks, at least the serious ones, it's become a lot easier to sound "too good."

Unfortunately, the industry seems to be lagging in this realization. While the prospect base demands truth and accuracy, the majority (but certainly not all) of MLM companies and distributors still seem bent on torturing the data to their advantage.

Here's an article that deals specifically with one particular very tortured statistic—recruiting figures.

How to Recruit 100 Distributors a Day, Every Day of the Week!

I was exploring the Internet jungle a few weeks ago when I stumbled on what appeared to be an open MLM forum. It had pretty much been taken over by distributors for one dominant opportunity, however. Dare any member from a subordinate MLM species wander into their domain, there would be a frenzy of activity to see who could convince the newcomer that their MLM program was superior—and from the looks of their online conversations, they were succeeding.

The lure wasn't the promise of quick and easy wealth, for there was actually little mention of high incomes. Nor was it the miraculous benefits of their amazing product line. Instead, they were trading recruiting figures. Massive recruiting figures.

One had recruited eleven people his first day in the business. Another claimed she built a downline of more than thirty-five hundred by her second month. Yet another claimed the company as a whole had gained more than 180,000 distributors since January. And yes, one even claimed he had "personally recruited one hundred people in a single day!"

This would all be very impressive—if I could pay my rent with distributor applications.

It's fascinating how the marketing trends in this industry evolve from year to year. In 1991 and 1992 everyone bragged about how much their top earners were making. In 1993 and 1994 everyone was hyping their company's total monthly sales or sales growth. And in the middle of this time span I remember a short-lived phase in which the age of a company seemed most important. Today, everyone's talking about how many distributors his or her company has. It seems we've now entered a phase where what is actually the least important factor is now considered the most important!

To create a marketing advantage, the "in" thing now seems to be how to redefine "distributor" to claim the highest possible number of them. For example, the previous MLM program and several others now entering make-believe momentum have a free sign-up system via an 800-number (In fact, in some of these programs, you can even sign up distributors without them knowing you did it.) So, retail customers now routinely sign up as "distributors" to get the product at wholesale.

Several companies now allow their distributors to sign up their spouse, or any family members, and some even allow you to sign yourself up as many times as you want! Others technically forbid such practices, but their distributors are doing it anyway and without consequence. So although the company may only gain two hundred actual distributors next month, it may be able to claim an increase of more than one thousand distributorships.

The technique is to simply give out sequential ID numbers to anyone who orders even a single product, one time, and to all the positions occupied by each distributor. Then, call each ID number a "distributor."

Another way to make sure that this number always increases is to never purge your inactive distributors. Technically, a company can't terminate a person for not ordering product (although MLM companies, like any direct sales company, can require a sales quota to earn commissions, they can't require a product purchase just to maintain distributor status). Instead, most will place non-ordering distributors in an "inactive" file and simply remove them from the distributor hierarchy. Some, however, will continue to count these people in their total distributor figure because they are, technically, still distributors.

Most MLM companies have some sort of annual renewal process in which a small administration fee is charged, or at least they have a reapplication process to weed out the dead wood. Of course, if you omit this process, and inactive distributors are still technically considered in the program, then essentially they are "distributors" for life! No matter how many quit, the "total distributor" figure will always be climbing. What's more, the company can now claim a "zero percent attrition rate!"

And it would be true—technically.

MLM programs that employ a binary compensation plan have a unique advantage in this area that's exclusively their own. In a binary, one person can potentially occupy numerous "income centers." I know of at least two such companies that are currently claiming a "total distributor" figure based on the total number of income centers. Fortunately, most of the binary plan contingent have not followed suit.

So here's the formula to build a "one-million distributor company" within five years:

1. Allow anyone to sign up for free, over the phone.
2. Count product customers as distributors, even if they only order once and you never hear from them again.
3. Allow them to sign up as many times as they want, or disallow it but look the other way.
4. Allow them to sign up any and all family members.
5. Never purge your company database of inactive distributors.

(Or, you can just not reveal your total distributor figure and just let your distributors "estimate." That should at least double the actual amount.)

Just imagine if Amway or Shaklee adopted the previous criteria when defining "distributor." They could easily claim to have one hundred million of them by now! I recently saw an ad for a popular MLM program with the headline "Over 250,000 people have joined (blank) International!" Of course, the ad doesn't mention that well over half of them are no longer distributors.

Semantics plays a very important role in the MLM industry today. By changing the standard definition of various aspects, companies today can create the illusion that they are in whatever stage of growth the company desires. Want to sound like a "ground floor opportunity?" Just say you're in "pre-launch"—

even if you're in your second year of business. Want to sound like a mature, stable company? Count all the years you thought about starting an MLM operation and then claim "ten years in development"—even if you launched yesterday. Want to sound like you're entering a massive momentum stage? Count every single person who contacts your company, for any reason, as a distributor—then heavily promote how many distributors are joining each month.

Several years ago, this same logic was used by the second baseman on my Little League team. After losing the final game of the season by a goodly margin, and all but three of the previous seventeen games, this curly-haired little seven-year-old attempted to comfort me by exclaiming, "Ya' know, coach, not counting the games we lost, we were *undefeated*!"

This also reminds me of the debate regarding whether legalizing drugs would affect the crime rate. Advocates of this idea claim the crime rate would drop dramatically. Of course it would! If you make fewer things illegal, they'll be fewer laws broken. Hey, why don't we just declare everything legal? Then we would have virtually no crime!

So, let's get to the big question: How can you, personally, recruit one hundred distributors a day, every day of the week? Simple. Get your company to employ the following recruiting system: You walk up to someone on the street, tap them on the shoulder twice with the index finger of your right hand, and say "I dub thee a distributor." That's it!

Think about the possibilities. You could literally recruit a thousand new distributors each day if you found a busy intersection in a major city. And if you trained just a handful of people in your downline to do the same, you could build an organization larger than ten thousand within days! And, of course, your company could easily claim to have more than one million distributors within just a few short weeks.

Now, understand, no one will make one thin dime in commissions. But remember, it's recruiting figures that count . . . Right?

* * *

In all modesty, I believe that *MarketWave* is the only company that has ever done a long-term statistical analysis of network marketing. I don't mean a quick survey here and there, but an ongoing, ever-increasing storehouse of MLM data. Unfortunately, most statistical data isn't worth a hill 'o bean counters unless you have a quantity of it. For example, Ty Cobb holds the Major League record for highest career batting average at .367, despite the fact that an outfielder for the Cleveland Indians by the name of Jackie Gallagher had a "one-thousand" career batting average! Of course, 'ol Jackie only got to bat once.

I recruited four of the first six people I ever prospected. Do you think I maintained that 67% recruiting ratio? No, it dropped a little after the next twenty-two straight prospects said "no."

So despite an ongoing effort to put the numbers together over the last six years, it was not until about January 1994 that we really had the numbers to say anything valid about the industry.

This information was derived from many sources, including formal surveys (passed out at all my Facts & Myths of MLM seminars around the country and published at least once a year in *MarketWave*), short mini-surveys found on the back of subscription renewal coupons, personal interviews (which we used to call "Survey Q's"), my personal database of more than nineteen thousand MLMers who have contacted me since October 1990, and approximately nine hundred pages of notes from all my telephone conversations over the last five-plus years.

Survey Results (And What They Mean)

This article was updated April 30, 1996.

Average age of distributor: 37.3 years. And rising! Professionals, white collar workers, vulnerable middle managers, and retired folks are discovering MLM. To put this in perspective, the average American is just over thirty-five years old.

Sex: Male, 51%; Female, 41%; Business/Trust, 4%; Couples, 4%   And the number of men are rising, perhaps because more of them fall into the categories listed in the section above. The female-oriented home party type MLMs are now rare, and many husband-and-wife teams are registered only under the man's name (however politically incorrect this may be). I'd guess that if you were to drop the number of men by 10% and increase "couples" by the same amount, you might get an even more accurate picture.

Primary reason for joining an MLM program

Reason	Men	Women	All
More money	61%	42%	49%
More free time	26%	34%	31%
Purchase products	6%	14%	11%
Other	7%	10%	9%

Actually, most responses did usually fall within these three general categories. "More money" responses included those that involved any material gain, such as "new house," or "retirement account." "More free time" responses included such goals as "waking up later," "spending more time with family," or "work at home/no more commuting." "Other" usually involved personal goals such as "security," "self-esteem," or "meet more people."

By the way, the majority of those who answered with just "more money," who were asked why they wanted to have more money usually said something to the effect of "to have more free time." This seems to be the real goal most MLM distributors are after—not money!

The discrepancy between men and women when it came to the goal of "more money" versus "more time" may not be as vast as it first appears. Men seemed to answer more from the gut, with the first thing that popped in their heads. Women seemed to see money more as a means to an end. They tended to answer more from the heart, with what they wanted to achieve with the money they earned. When men were pressed to think more about their desire for more money, the freedom angle really attracted them as well. I suspect it might actually be at about the same percentage as women.

Years in MLM: 3.1 Admittedly, we may be responsible for some unintentional data torturing here. Well, more like data irritating actually. Those who would respond to a written survey, which is where most of the data for this question came from, are likely to be a more serious, thus more committed, group overall. I suspect this number might actually be slightly lower. Also, note that this is an average, not a mean. In other words, a few had been in for ten or twenty years, whereas most had been in for less than three.

MLM participation by state (percentage of people within each state who are MLM distributors)

Top Ten	Bottom Ten
Nevada, 4.68%	Iowa, 0.03%
Hawaii, 4.18	W. Virginia, 0.08
Florida, 4.11	Georgia, 1.01
Colorado, 3.92	Mississippi, 1.04
Arizona, 3.87	S. Dakota, 1.08
Utah, 3.76	Delaware, 1.17
Washington, 3.15	Nebraska, 1.26
Oregon, 3.09	Kentucky, 1.37
Arkansas, 3.03	Vermont, 1.39
Massachusetts, 2.98	Maine, 1.45

We did more than just define what states had the most MLM distributors. Obviously, the larger states such as California and Texas would come out on top. Instead, we determined what percentage of all MLM distributors were in each state (based on a survey of more than six thousand distributors), then figured what the total number of distributors was in that state, and finally, what percentage of that state's population were MLM distributors. This gives us a better idea of which states are hot and cold MLM states. The obvious conclusion: Go west!

By the way, Texas came in eleventh with 2.76%, and California was sixteenth with 2.55%. New York was thirty-seventh with 2.35%.

Average total distributors recruited in MLM career: 2.1   Here is one of the biggest statistical fallacies in this industry. I've heard other figures ranging from 2.6 to as high as 3. Unfortunately, we fall victim to the same bias as all others who have tried to determine this number. First, we are only surveying current, active distributors. As I mentioned earlier, if everyone who ever participated in MLM over the last fifty years recruited just an even two, we would have reached worldwide saturation. Also, considering the number of people who participate in two or more programs at once (or who've been in dozens over the years), many of those 2.1 are undoubtedly the same people getting counted more than once. Furthermore, determining an "average" creates the illusion that most or all distributors are recruiting about two or three people. In fact, more than half of all MLM distributors never recruit a soul, and drop out within weeks. Many recruit just one. Very few recruit exactly two people. What causes this average to reach higher than the 2.0 level are those very few who recruit four, five, ten, twenty or perhaps more than one hundred people.

This is why any program that hypes this "If you get two, who only get two" routine, whether it be a two-wide matrix or an Australian (two-up), is using faulty logic. The chances are, the two you get won't get anybody. Also, you won't get any spillover unless you happen to fall under one of those very few who recruit more than two. And the few you do get from spillover, if any, will likely recruit—that's right—no one! Yes, the "average" may be two for all those surveyed, but the most common numbers actually recruited are one—and none.

Actually, it is technically impossible for the recruitment "average" of all distributors to be greater than one. Let's say you are the very first MLM distributor. You recruit two people. There are now three distributors and two recruits. That's an average of 0.67. Now the two you recruit also recruit two. So now seven MLM distributors have recruited a total of six recruits, but the "average" is only 0.86. Even if every new recruit were to continue to recruit two others, this average would only proceed to get closer and closer to, but never reaching, one-point-zero.

Average number of MLM programs pursued in career: 3.9 You might be surprised at this low number. I certainly was. I found that there were many distributors who were still with their first or second company, however, and only a few who had been with several. Those few just seemed to stand out more because they tended to be either well-known veterans of MLM, or junkies who had been in dozens of programs. Actually, we found that most new distributors just didn't hang around long enough to involve themselves with more than one company.

On a scale of 1 to 5 (5 being the highest, 3 meaning indifferent, 1 meaning you hate it), various types of product lines were rated like this:

Health Care: 4.09	Pet Care: 2.89
Skin Care: 3.86	Publications: 2.74
Cookies/Foods: 3.51	Water/Air Purifiers: 2.61
Weight Loss: 3.29	Automotive: 2.58*
Hair care: 3.23	MLM Portfolios: 2.55
Gold/Jewelry: 3.21	Tax/Record Keeping: 2.41
Dental/Medical: 3.187	Telecommunications: 2.36
Educational: 3.185	Lead Generation: 2.32
Cosmetics: 3.15	Toys/Games: 1.78
Benefits Packages: 2.99	Downline Builders: 1.66
Travel: 2.90*	Chain Letters: 1.00

Recent additions to survey—figures based on less than 100 responses.

Notice that Chain Letters never received even one rating of higher than a 1. I'm impressed, but a little skeptical too. Does this mean no one would ever participate in one, or they have and failed miserably with it?

Of course, the real question here is: do distributors claim to prefer skin/hair/health care lines because that's what the company they're involved in sells, or are they involved with these companies because they sell the products they prefer?

What seems to be obvious is that Discovery Toys distributors need to participate in more MLM surveys.

Number of MLM programs pursued at the same time:

One: 51%
Two: 29%
Three: 13%
Four: 4%
Five or more: 3%

Record for most opportunities pursued in career: 36   And this guy is still looking, by the way.

Record for most opportunities pursued at the same time: 18 And she's quite proud of it.

Percent of total MLM companies that offer each type of compensation plan (see Compensation Plan Terms in the Appendix for a brief description of each type of plan):

Break-Away: 61%
Unilevel: 18%
Binary: 11%
Matrix: 8%
Australian (Two-Up): 1%
Hybrid/Unknown: 1%

Despite the doomsday predictions of some break-away bashers, the ol' stair-step has only dropped 7% over the last five years. However, 85% of all companies older than seven years are break-aways, so either there was a dip somewhere or break-aways just tend to last longer. Matrix plans have also dropped, likely a result of the increase in popularity of the binary plan, which is actually a form of matrix (they hate it when I say that). Besides the binary, only the unilevel seems to be gaining a slow but steady increase in popularity. Fortunately, Australian plans have never exceeded 1% since I've been keeping track.

Number of total MLM distributors (United States only): 6,936,700   A far cry from the ten-to-fifteen million we keep hearing about. I computed this figure by adding up all the distributor totals for each of the 313 companies in my database (about half are estimates, but they're close estimates). These are the 313 most prominent companies and do not include any who are less than six months old. I then assumed, very optimistically, that there were two hundred more companies with an average of one thousand distributors each. I have also added quasi-MLM operations such as Avon and Tupperware to the mix. I did everything I could, within reason, to justify the "fifteen million distributor" claim. I didn't torture the data, I made love to it! And I couldn't even come close to ten-to-fifteen million.

What is even more revealing is that the top 2.5% of all MLM companies (by size) comprises 68% of all the distributors! These companies averaged 464,100 distributors each, whereas the other 97.5% of companies averaged only 5,717 distributors.

Actual number of current MLM distributors: 4,655,000   The most scathing evidence against the "fifteen million" claim is that 49% of all network marketers are currently enrolled in more than one MLM program, so we are actually counting about 2.3 million of these folks more than once!

Top ten states where MLM companies are based, with number located within each:

1. California: 66
2. Texas: 40
3. Florida: 28
4. Utah: 20
5. Arizona: 12
6. Illinois: 10
7. Nevada: 10
8. New York: 9
9. Ohio: 8
10. Washington: 8

Oldest MLM Companies:
1. Shaklee: 40 years
2. Neo-Life: 38 years
3. Amway: 37 years
4. Mary Kay: 33 years
5. NSA: 27 years

Number of MLM companies (past and present) whose name ends with "way": 8   Can you name them?

Number of MLM companies whose name starts with these letters of the alphabet:
  A: 33
  B: 19
  C: 32

Okay, I'm getting ridiculous. Obviously, I've hit the bottom of the barrel as far as MLM-related statistics are concerned.

Conclusion

I suspect the majority of you reading this book are already involved in network marketing. You are the intended audience. Some of you, however, may have picked up this book as part of your research into MLM—to assist you in deciding whether to join this industry or not. Although not every page was filled with "happy stuff," I certainly hope I have not dissuaded you from pursuing a good MLM venture. If anything, I hope you have recognized the tremendous potential that network marketing has to improve the lives of millions of Americans—including yours. I hope you now understand and appreciate that we've only scratched the surface of that potential. And most of all, I hope you now understand why.

This book is not about why you should abandon or avoid network marketing. It is about why you should embrace it, love it, support it, respect it, teach it, and help it grow up into the awesome, literally world-changing marvel that it could be. This book is about doing the business, but doing it with awareness and understanding with realistic expectations. It's about doing the business, but doing it with honesty, integrity, and fairness. It's all about doing the business, but doing it right!

Is there a "perfect" MLM opportunity? Probably not. Is there a good, honest program that's trying hard to do right, with a fair compensation plan and good products that are worth the price? Absolutely. Dozens of them.

Other publications, agencies, and organizations can assist you in determining which MLM companies fall into this category. Of course, one good way of determining which opportunities have the least to hide is by judging their acceptance and support of this book! If an MLM distributor handed you this copy, you can pretty much assume his or her opportunity is one of the good ones.

Should you try to find a perfect MLM opportunity? I hope not—unless you're very young. It might take awhile. But if you can find one that's even close, I'll bet you can make it close to perfect for you. Do you hate front-loading? Fine. Don't front-load anybody. Do you hate deceptive opportunity presentations? Don't give them. Do you object to ridiculous medical or income claims? Don't make them. Are you afraid of filling up your garage with unwanted product? Don't buy that much. And you know, being a business of duplication and all, your downline just might follow your example. You see, we are in control of the destiny of network marketing in this country. We can choose to make this business a safer, more dignified, far more rewarding opportunity for average, struggling Americans.

Some of you grizzled veterans of MLM may be thinking, Len, it's just not that simple.

Well, actually, I think it is.

Resources

Subscription Publications

MLM Insider
1521 Alton Road, Ste. 157
Miami, FL 33139

Fortune Now
PO Box 890084
Houston, TX 77289

Upline Journal
400 E. Jefferson
Charlottesville, VA 22902

Profit Now
(previously published by MarketWave)
7342 N. Ivanhoe Avenue
Fresno, CA 93722

Other Industry Trade Publications

Cutting Edge Opportunities
1250 Ridge Road
Elizabethtown, PA 17022

Emerald Coast News
PO Box 190
Niceville, FL 32588

Money & Profits
39 Bowery Street, #919
New York, NY 10002

Money Maker's Monthly
6827 W. 171st Street
Tinley Park, IL 60477

The Network Trainer
PO Box 890084
Houston, TX 77289

Profit$
PO Box 4785
Lincoln, NE 68504

Trade Organizations

Direct Selling Association
1776 K Street, NW, Ste. 600
Washington, DC 20006

MLMIA
119 Stanford Court
Irvine, CA 92715

PANM
2815 S. Alma School Road, Ste. 119
Mesa, AZ 85210

Productivity Tools

Carson Services
(Fax-On-Demand Service)
PO Box 4395
Lincoln, NE 68504

GenePro
(Downline Tracking Software)
Target Data Corporation
8-A Village Loop, Suite 220
Pomona, CA 91766

PowerLine Systems
(Planner/Organizer)
151 Kalmus Drive, Ste. C-260
Costa Mesa, CA 92626

General MLM Support Services

FirstNet
PO Box 4395
Lincoln, NE 68504

L.A.N.T. System
50 Follen Street, Ste. 507
Cambridge, MA 02138

Marketing Consultant

Randy Gage
1680 Michigan Avenue, Ste. 1036
Miami Beach, FL 33139

Advertising Consultant

Opportunity Connection
17319 Crystal Valley Road
Little Rock, AR 72210

MLM Start-Up Consultant

Leonard Clements
800-688-4766
(see pages 28–32 before calling)

Graphics & Design

TechnoGraphics
PO Box 4324
Lincoln, NE 68504

Compensation Plan Terms

Australian Unlimited first-level width, infinite depth, linear commissions.

This is usually referred to in the United States as a "two-up" plan. The commissions earned by the first two distributors on your first level are passed up to your sponsor. Likewise, the commission from the first two distributors recruited by your third recruit (and on) are passed up to you.

Binary First-level width always limited to two, infinite depth, generational commissions. Sometimes referred to as a Binary Lateral. This plan determines commission payments based on the accumulated sales volume in each of the two legs (group volume under each of the two first-level distributors) usually on a weekly basis. Little consideration is given to actual levels, only the total volume in each leg. The more volume that occurs during the week, the higher the commission payment. Most binary plans pay based on the leg with the least volume and the excess volume in the strong leg is either carried over to the following week or "flushed" (forfeited). Binary plans generally allow multiple positions by a single distributor.

Break-Away Unlimited first-level width, finite depth (usually four to seven levels), generational commissions.

When a certain stage of advancement has been reached, based on various qualifications usually involving monthly wholesale personal and group volumes, the distributor and his or her group (downline) "breaks away" from their upline sponsor. This process usually involves eliminating the break-away group's volume as a source of volume in meeting the upline sponsor's monthly qualifications. Commissions (usually called overrides) can still be earned on this break-away group once an equivalent or higher stage of advancement has been reached by the upline sponsor.

Downline All of those distributors who are within your personal organization. They all branch off from your position in a downward direction.

Generational commissions Commissions are based on the group volume of the distributor on that level. For example, if a break-away plan paid 5% on

169

level six, this would include the entire group volume of the level six distributor, not just the volume that occurs on the sixth level. This group volume rarely, if ever, includes the volume of other break-away groups.

Linear commissions Commissions are based on the actual volume that occurs on that specific level.

Matrix Limited first-level width (usually two to seven positions), finite depth (usually five to twelve levels), linear commissions.

Usually all volume that falls within the pay levels counts toward monthly qualifications. Matrix plans are described by the first-level width limit and the number of levels. For example, a 2x12 (no more than two distributors may be placed on your first level, and the plan pays twelve levels deep). All distributors enrolled beyond the first level width limit are placed in deeper levels. This is commonly referred to as "spillover."

Stair-Step Any type of plan that has multiple stages or ranks of advancement. For example: Bronze, Gold, and Diamond, or Member, Leader, and Director, and so on. Although any of these plan types can be designated a stair-step, this term rarely precedes any type of plan other than break-away. All break-aways are "stair-step" break-aways.

Unilevel Unlimited first-level width, finite depth (usually five to nine levels), linear commissions. Generally the simplest form of plan. No break-away occurs and an unlimited number of distributors can be placed on any level. The term was originally used to describe any type of plan that had only one (uni-) stage (level) of advancement (compared with a stair-step of ranks that could be achieved). Today it is commonly used to describe any non-matrix, non-break-away type of plan regardless of the number of ranks or stages of advancement.

Upline The direct line of distributors who are above you in the hierarchy.

Recommended Reading

Here are some (but not all) of my favorite MLM books.

Being the Best You Can Be in MLM, by John Kalench. MIM Publications, San Diego, CA, 1990.

Big Al Tells All, by Tom Schreiter. KAAS Publishing, Houston, TX, 1985.

Congratulations, You Lost Your Job!, by Beverly Nadler. MLM Publishing, Charlottesville, VA, 1992.

Financially Free, by Dennis Windsor. Windward Press, Dallas, TX, 1990.

How to Create a Recruiting Explosion, by Tom Schreiter. KAAS Publishing, Houston, TX, 1986.

MLM Magic, by Venus Andrecht. Ransom Hill Press, Ramona, CA, 1992.

Network Marketer's Guide to Success, by J. Babener and D. Stewart. Legaline Publications, Portland, OR, 1990.

Power Calling, by Joan Guiducci. Tonino, Mill Valley, CA, 1992.

Power MLM, by Mark Yarnell. MYD Publications, Austin, TX, 1990.

Romancing Your Future, by Philip Stills. Philip Stills Business Books, Santa Rosa, CA, 1994.

Street Smart Networking, by Robert Butwin. MLM Publishing, Charlottesville, VA, 1994.

The Greatest Networker in the World, by John Milton Fogg. MLM Publishing, Charlottesville, VA, 1992.

Turbo MLM, by Tom Schreiter. KAAS Publishing, Houston, TX, 1988.

Wave Three: The New Era in Network Marketing, by Richard Poe. Prima Publishing, Rocklin, CA, 1993.

Who Stole the American Dream?, by Burke Hedges. INTI Publications, Tampa, FL, 1993.

Winning the Greatest Game of All, by Randy Ward. Cimarron Management Corporation, Jennings, OK, 1990.

About the Author

Leonard Clements was born and raised in San Anselmo, California, just north of San Francisco. He attended Sir Francis Drake High School, where he graduated with honors while finishing in the top 10% in the nation in mathematics. After attending one year of college, he decided to "take a semester off." Six years later he returned to earn his degree in Business Data Processing.

Len's MLM career began in 1979 with a health and nutrition company that, six months later (the same week that he gave notice at his job) went out of business. Len did get his job back, but that swift feeling of success had lit the entrepreneurial fire within him (or, as his original partners in *MarketWave* told him, made him "psychologically unemployable").

After a short stint with two other failed MLM companies, he decided to go the conventional route and opened a computer training and time rental facility in downtown San Francisco. After six profitable years of business (despite numerous thefts, car break-ins, a drug raid on an adjoining business, a suicide outside the front door, two drive-by shootings, and a major earthquake), Len had had enough of "The City."

Len spent a full year doing his homework before re-entering the MLM arena, and soon discovered that there was a ready and willing market for that same knowledge. He held his first Facts & Myths of MLM seminar in his computer classroom in September 1990. Those seminars were a success and soon became a twice monthly event, each time selling out the room.